Umbrella Guide to

Ports of Call of
Southeast Alaska

by
Sherry Simpson

Best wishes,
Sherry Simpson

UMBRELLA BOOKS T.M.

An imprint of Epicenter Press

Editor: B.G. Olson
Cover design: Elizabeth Watson
Cover photo: Jeff Schultz, AlaskaStock Images
Maps: Scott Penwell
Pre-press production: Leslie Newman, Flora Wong, J. Stephen Lay
Printer: McNaughton & Gunn

© 1993 Sherry Simpson
ISBN 0-945397-19-4

To order single copies of
**UMBRELLA GUIDE TO
PORTS OF CALL OF SOUTHEAST ALASKA,**
send $12.95 (Washington residents add $1.06 state sales tax)
plus $3.05 for shipping to: Epicenter Press,
18821 64th Ave. N.E., Seattle, WA 98155.
Ask for our catalog. BOOKSELLERS: Retail discounts are available
from our trade distributor, Graphic Arts Center Publishing Co.,
Portland, OR, call 800-452-3032.

PRINTED IN THE UNITED STATES OF AMERICA
First printing, April, 1993

TABLE OF CONTENTS

INTRODUCTION

On the map, Southeast Alaska appears almost as an after thought to the vast bulk of Alaska. A slender strip composed more of islands than mainland, it is officially known as the Alexander Archipelago. Over the years, more than one nickname has attached itself to this ramble of northern territory: the Panhandle, the Banana Belt, the Inside Passage.

The Inside Passage is perhaps most apt, for to slip through this chain of islands is to journey into another world. If Alaska is a state, the Inside Passage is a state of mind. Here the ocean is everything. The tide clocks the passing of the days. The seas mark the mercurial weather. The waves batter and caress the coast. The depths yield salmon, halibut, herring, crab, and a multitude of creatures great and small. The fiords and straits isolate one town from another.

The Tlingit Indians depended upon and celebrated the ocean's bounty long before voyagers, explorers, and adventurers sailed these waters, thinking they had discovered something new. These new arrivals scattered the charts with Spanish, Russian, British, and American names. Today, as the most recent of explorers, you may find yourself just as overwhelmed by a sense of discovery.

As you cruise north through the maze of inlets, straits and channels, the Pacific Ocean lurks to the west beyond the protective barrier of islands. To the east, the Coast Range dominates the horizon and marks the border of Canada. The ocean and mountains form a meteorological tag team that tempers the weather into an even mildness, creating cool summers, warm winters, and, by the way, rain. Lots of rain.

Truth be told, some people believe it's only the rain that prevents Southeast Alaska from being heralded as a bona fide paradise. The trick is not to think of Southeast as damp, dank or dark, but to admire the way the clouds wreath the mountain tops, to appreciate the ethereal light, to relish the misty panorama. If not for the rain, Southeast Alaska would not be carpeted with the luxuriant green velvet of the coastal rain forest, nor seamed with glistening plaits of streams and rivers that host the salmon that feed so many. The color scheme is gray and green, blue and silver, and all shades in between.

Two communities inhabit this territory. The wildlife population includes humpback and orca whales, brown and black bears, Sitka black-tailed deer, Dall and harbor porpoises, sea lions, seals, and a host of smaller creatures. The human population clusters in more than a dozen towns and villages floating on islands or tucked into coves, bights, and channels. With 11,000 miles of coastline squeezed into a stretch of territory just 500 miles long, there are endless variations on the predominant theme of mountain, forest and ocean.

The main routes are often called the marine highway, for just cause. Even the aviation age has not eliminated the shipping traffic along these waterways. Vessels of all sizes and character travel these routes. In a single day on the wide straits you may pass barges, fishing boats, lumber freighters, ore ships, tugboats nudging log rafts, sailboats, skiffs, and yachts. Few sights are prettier than the great cruise ships rumbling by at night with lights aglow like a floating chandelier. Few sights are more welcome than the arrival of the Alaska Marine Highway's "blue canoes," the state ferries that bind Southeasterners together.

These modern-day ships represent the latest chapter in the big book of maritime history, which begins with the proud, seafaring Tlingit canoes and continues on to the grand sailing ships of explorers, the shabby skiffs of prospectors, and the purposeful steamers linking Southeast Alaska with the world.

You are part of that history, too. Beginning in the 1880s, curious travelers cruised through the Inside Passage on steamships, eager to visit frontier towns and admire scenic beauty. A century later, visitors seek the same experiences, although today's traveler quickly realizes that the modern world has discovered Alaska, too. Fast food, cable television, and shopping malls have invaded the larger towns. Fortunately, many of the old mine relics, totem poles, saloons, and Victorian buildings remain steadfastly sheltered from progress. Likewise, most of the wilderness still hoards its treasures of alpine lakes, glaciers, hidden valleys, mountain trails and pristine coastline. Wildlife does not exist behind bars here; it roams all about where it will, in skies, sea and forest.

In the early days, naturalist John Muir complained about "armchair tourists" more interested in buying trinkets and complaining about their rough surroundings than appreciating Alaska's wonders. You, of course, are a different sort of traveler, or you wouldn't be reading this or any other guide. Just bear in mind that every town in Southeast, from Ketchikan to Skagway, wears its own distinctive history and harbors its own quirky personality. You have only to open your eyes to see the real Southeast Alaska. We hope this book helps as you make your ports of call along the Inside Passage.

Ketchikan

Ketchikan is a town of many faces, making it an ideal introduction to Southeast Alaska. Steeped in Native culture, it is also a center of commerce. Here the past speaks through the remarkable collections of totem poles and other artifacts preserved as legacies of the Tlingit, Haida and Tsimshian nations. But as the state's fourth-largest town with 14,000 people, the community also reflects the brash nature of those who came looking for the future in the area's abundant natural resources. Though younger than nearly all of Southeast's major communities, Ketchikan claims the largest number of surviving historic structures in the state. This cultural chowder means that here you can soak in the timelessness of a Tlingit tribal house, stay in a turn-of-the-century hotel, and browse through a modern shopping mall.

Fish, minerals, and timber fueled the success of Alaska's so-called "First City" — so much so that during one period the town was first not only in geographic position but in population, surpassing even Juneau, Fairbanks, and Anchorage. But Ketchikan's greatest natural resource, as the joke goes, is rain. More than 150 inches of liquid sunshine falls here each year; just think of it as 12 feet. At least once before leaving you'll hear the local weather forecast: "If you can't see the top of Deer Mountain, it's raining. If you can see it, it's about to rain."

With its tangle of pilings, stairways and boardwalks, the town seems perched on stilts. Houses and buildings creep along the waterfront and up the slopes like vines yearning for room to grow. It's said that Ketchikan is three miles long and three blocks wide. That's not strictly true, of course, but you are never far from the sea here. Tongass Avenue snakes along the

1

waterfront to parallel Tongass Narrows — a channel so slender, in fact, that visitors sometimes mistake it for a river. Nearby Pennock Island and Gravina Island nestle close to the island upon which Ketchikan is planted, Revillagigedo. No need to twist your tongue; locals settle for "Revilla."

Despite its "there's work to be done" aura, when the cruise ships leave, Ketchikan unmasks itself as thoroughly small-time Alaska. Cheers and shouts float through the air from the ballpark. On historic Front Street, music spills out of the Fo'c'sle Bar as laughing fishermen wander next door to the Totem Bar. Just beyond Thompson Basin boat harbor, an angler strains to net a struggling king salmon, the boat wobbling with his effort.

At one time Ketchikan was heralded as the "Canned Salmon Capital of the World." The gleaming run of spawning salmon filling Ketchikan Creek inspired Irishman Mike Martin in 1885 to buy 160 acres of creek and waterfront land for a salmon cannery here. Martin, a "salmon prospector" sent from Oregon to look for such a site near the region's rich fishing grounds, was not the first to recognize the creek's true wealth. According to Ketchikan historian Mary Balcom, a Tlingit named "Kitschk" was there fishing in summer camp long before any white people arrived. (Kitschk's name translates as "thundering wings of an eagle.") The Tlingits named the creek "Kitschk-hin," meaning "Kitschk's stream." White men corrupted the name to "Kitskan" and eventually "Ketchikan" (pronounced "Catch-a-can").

Martin believed the site would become the fishing center of Alaska. He was right. Soon canneries, salteries, trading posts, saloons, missionaries and others gathered around the creek and surrounding areas. In 1900, the city was incorporated and Mike Martin elected mayor.

The town also fed on discoveries of gold, silver, lead, copper, and marble on Prince of Wales Island and elsewhere, making Ketchikan both a mining and fishing center. But fishing was the mainstay, particularly as the minerals market declined. Imagine how the town revolved around fishing early in the century. By 1922, there were 32 canneries in the area. Chinese cannery workers (and later Filipinos and Japanese) spent long hours packing salmon. Fishermen, many of them Scandinavian, headed out to sea in dories after halibut and salmon. The waterfront filled with packing plants and warehouses, wharves and freezing plants, mechanics, metalsmiths and boat builders. A spruce mill sprung up to produce boxes for packaging cans. A 1930 headline in the Ketchikan Alaska Chronicle tells it all: "More

2

Canned Salmon is Packed in Ketchikan Than in Any Other City in the World." Millions of pounds of halibut, too, were iced, boxed, and shipped to Seattle.

The fish couldn't last forever, something the packers recognized immediately by fostering hatcheries. But hatcheries couldn't keep up with such efficient methods as the fish trap, which collected salmon in such devastating numbers (one trap alone gathering 400,000 in 24 hours) that the devices were banned when Alaska achieved statehood.

It was too late. The salmon fisheries collapsed so severely in the 1940s and 1950s that President Dwight Eisenhower later named the region a disaster area. The loss of both the fishing and mining industries in Southeast after World War II meant communities like Ketchikan needed some other way to sustain themselves. Ketchikan's salvation proved to be the Ketchikan Pulp Mill.

With a 50-year contract with the U.S. Forest Service guaranteeing a cheap supply of lumber from the Tongass National Forest, the $53 million mill opened in 1954 at nearby Ward Cove. The company quickly became the economic force behind Ketchikan, as it is to this day. Building the mill added about 4,500 people to the local population, resulting in more roads, homes, schools, and so on. Today the company says the plant contributes 1,000 year-around jobs at logging camps, sawmills and the mill to produce pulp, paper pulp and lumber. (Tours of the mill are available for those over 12; call 225-2151 for the schedule.)

Tourism and other businesses gild the city's economy today. A revitalized fishing industry now focuses largely on fresh and frozen products, though several canneries still operate. The fishing culture is evident everywhere, not only on the wharves, but in places such as the public radio station, which offers a music show called "Babblefish," and in the quirky fish artwork and T-shirt designs of Ketchikan artist Ray Troll. Fishing built Ketchikan, and Ketchikan keeps building on fishing.

Attractions

Though the main road, Tongass Highway, rambles along the shoreline of Revillagigedo for some 31 miles, the sights of the downtown area lie within pleasant walking distance of each other.

3

Downtown Ketchikan is a hybrid of the historical and the commercial. The Visitors Bureau, located on the Cruise Ship Dock, can point you in the right direction with brochures, information, and a well-detailed walking map. Should you bypass the numerous guided tours in favor of exploring on your own, head up Dock or Mission streets and look for the distinctive replica of the Chief Johnson Totem Pole, distinguished by the "fabulous bird," Kadjuk, soaring at the top. When the original pole dating to 1901 was removed in 1982 to the Totem Heritage Center, several skeletons believed to be sacrificed slaves were discovered underneath. A favorite photo stop, the pole marks the nearby Tongass Historical Museum or the entrance to Creek Street.

At the Tongass Historical Museum you'll discover you are in good company. Since the late 19th century, when steamships began carrying tourists through the Inside Passage, visitors have enjoyed gawking at Ketchikan's totem poles, buying souvenirs, and marveling at salmon runs up Ketchikan Creek. Other exhibits explain early life in Ketchikan and the region's history of commercial fishing. A 12-foot model of a purse seiner, the *Ketchikan Queen*, presents a close-up look at a fishing boat. You can also learn how fish are processed from "catch to can."

The museum reminds visitors of the region's original inhabitants with an explanation of the Tlingit, Haida and Tsimshian peoples and examples of stone tools, carving, crests, and items from communal house interiors. This display offers the best exhibit in Southeast of Native subsistence foods.

A guided tour schedule is posted weekly. The museum is open daily in summers for a small admission. Entrance is free on Sunday afternoons. Call 225-5600.

Some fishermen claim Ketchikan has the toughest bars in Southeast. If true, that's only the latest mark of distinction in the town's rowdy social history, remembered today at Creek Street, the site of Ketchikan's red light district. Just about every town in Alaska had a street where ladies of the night earned a living, but no other city owns up to it with such pride, though early town leaders were not particularly proud of what Judge James Wickersham once called the "Barbary Coast of the North." The historic district greatly resembles its origins in 1903, when town leaders shooed all the bawdy houses to one convenient location near the harbor. A boardwalk community lining the banks of Ketchikan Creek, Creek Street was known

4

as the "only place in the world where both the fish and the fishermen go upstream to spawn." The district closed in the early 1950s after scandal engulfed the government and police department.

Today Creek Street remains just as colorful and a lot more respectable, with gift stores, art galleries, curio shops and restaurants offering everything from chili to Chinese food. To return to the old days, you need only step into No. 24, known as Dolly's House. This tiny clapboard home was the home of "Big Dolly Arthur." Now a private museum, Dolly's place captures the life of one of Creek Street's more infamous characters. Guided tours are available for a small fee.

Though the madams and customers are long gone, you can still watch the salmon head upstream in Ketchikan Creek. A 15-minute stroll from the museum area to City Park provides several vantage points of salmon battling up the creek's fish ladder to spawning grounds. In June though mid-August, look for big king salmon. From July to early August, the smaller salmon with humps on their backs are pink salmon. In September, expect a few cohos, or silver salmon.

The Deer Mountain Fish Hatchery, located at the park, shows visitors the early years of the salmon life cycle with its holding tanks of fingerlings and smolts. Built in 1954, the hatchery is owned by the City of Ketchikan and operated by the Alaska Department of Fish and Game. Displays and views of the hatchery's operations explain how the staff collect and fertilize eggs from returning salmon to rear over 600,000 juvenile salmon, steelhead and rainbow trout for release into natural habitats. Should you find yourself growing fond of the baby coho salmon, the hatchery has a fund-raising "adopt-a-salmon" program. ("No diapers to wash, no losing sleep," the program advertises.)

City Park is a pleasant place to picnic under the stately spruce and hemlock, to rest your feet or to enjoy the restored fountain. The ponds here were once used for an early hatchery.

Across the bridge is the Totem Heritage Center, a repository of Native cultural history and a remarkable collection of original totem poles. A three-year project ending in 1970 salvaged 33 poles, house posts and fragments from rotting away at nearby abandoned Haida and Tlingit villages. Built by the city in 1976, the museum is now listed on the National Register of Historic Places.

Five poles stand below the skylight through which they were lowered into the building. Worn by weather and time, they still exude an aura of power and mystery. The red cedar poles range from 101 to 156 years old. Guides can explain the purpose and stories of each pole. Also displayed are fine examples of spruce root baskets and other items. Contemporary artists work in a demonstration room amid the sweet odor of aging cedar emanating from nearby stored poles and fragments. The center also offers lectures and classes in Native arts. Works by Native artisans are sold in the gift shop. The museum is open daily with a small admission fee. Entrance is free Sunday afternoons. Call 225-5900.

Few can resist the tram ride from Creek Street up the hillside to the Westmark Cape Fox Lodge, with its superior vista from Boston Smith Hill, named for an early boxer. If you prefer your views with a dose of aerobic exercise, make a detour from Park Avenue up the stairway at Upland Way. (Even the stairways have street signs here.) After climbing 125 steps, passing homes perched along the way, you'll look down from a platform upon Creek Street, Pennock Island, and Thomas Basin boat harbor. Before

At high tide, Thomas Basin fills up to the pilings in Ketchikan.

6

the harbor was dredged in the 1930s, baseball games were played on the tidal flats when the tide was out.

Or head north on Front Street, cross the street and take the 100 or so stairs climbing the ridge next to the tunnel, burrowed in 1954 and supposedly the only tunnel in the world you can drive through, around, and over. The walkway is still technically Front Street, even though you're now on a boardwalk jutting over the hillside. This panorama affords a fine view of the waterfront, Tongass Narrows and the northern stretch of the city.

Take Pine Street over to its intersection with Main Street for a study in cultural contrasts. The replica totem pole commemorates Chief George Kyan, who sold property on Ketchikan Street to Mike Martin, leading to the town's founding. Touching the pole is said to bring luck. (Some say it brings money within 24 hours, but that's lucky, too.) Next to the pole is the historic Monrean House, the only surviving example of the Queen Anne style once popular here. Built in 1904 for one of the founders of the power company that later became the Ketchikan Spruce Mill, the house is now listed on the National Register of Historic Places.

As if the Totem Heritage Center and scattered totem poles weren't enough introduction to Alaska's first peoples, two outlying sites celebrate local Native history. Totem Bight State Historic Park, at 10 Mile North Tongass Highway, preserves a collection of 14 replica Tlingit and Haida totem poles and a representative clan house created in the 1930s by the Alaska Civilian Conservation Corps. A short path leads through the forest and among the totems as they face toward the sea. This is the only Alaska state park devoted solely to Native culture. The site is thought to have once been a Tlingit fish camp. Local tours usually include the park.

Saxman Village, at Mile 2.5 South Tongass Highway, celebrates Native culture and arts with a special authenticity. Saxman is more than a tourist destination. The community has its own government and serves as headquarters of the Cape Fox Corporation. The village itself was named after Samuel Saxman, a white teacher who taught school at Loring in 1886 but disappeared during an expedition to find a new joint community site for Tongass and Cape Fox villagers. Eight years later, the villagers chose this spot.

The tour includes a totem park featuring more than two dozen poles, some as much as a century old, that were retrieved from abandoned villages. Also located here is the Beaver Clan tribal house where dances are

7

performed, a carving center where master carvers create new poles, a multi-media theater, and an old school house. Potlatches and other celebrations are still held when a new pole is raised. This is a good place to appreciate how much work and craftsmanship go into the imposing totems. Look for artwork by Nathan Jackson, one of the state's finest and best-known Tlingit artists.

The village visitor center is open daily throughout the summer. Admission is free but guided tours require a fee. Call the center at 225-8687.

Visitor Information

Ketchikan Visitors Bureau on the cruise ship dock has brochures, video, coffee, a walking tour map, and helpful staff. Write: 131-FA Front St., Ketchikan, 99901 or call 225-6166.

The Greater Ketchikan Chamber of Commerce address is P.O. Box 5957, Ketchikan, 99901, or call 225-3184.

The Alaska Division of State Parks office is located at Totem Bight State Historical Park, Mile 10 North Tongass Highway, or call 247-8574.

The U.S. Forest Service Ketchikan Ranger District office has displays, films, maps, and information on campground sites, remote cabins and other recreation areas at 3031 Tongass Ave., Ketchikan, 99901, or call 225-2148.

The Alaska Department of Fish and Game has hunting and fishing regulations in the Tongass Commercial Center, 2030 Sea Level Drive. Call 225-2859.

The *Ketchikan Daily News* distributes the free *Ketchikan Guide* each summer with articles and advertisements on visitor services and attractions. Stop by 501 Dock St., write to P.O. Box 7900-V, Ketchikan, 99901 or call 225-3157.

Transportation

Ketchikan is called the "First City" because it is the first major port of call in Southeast Alaska. Like most other communities, it can be reached only by air or water.

The Alaska Marine Highway System terminal is located on North Tongass Highway about 2 miles north of downtown Ketchikan. Motels,

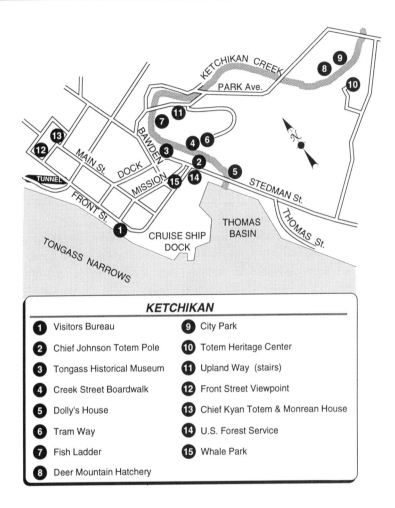

KETCHIKAN

1	Visitors Bureau	9	City Park
2	Chief Johnson Totem Pole	10	Totem Heritage Center
3	Tongass Historical Museum	11	Upland Way (stairs)
4	Creek Street Boardwalk	12	Front Street Viewpoint
5	Dolly's House	13	Chief Kyan Totem & Monrean House
6	Tram Way	14	U.S. Forest Service
7	Fish Ladder	15	Whale Park
8	Deer Mountain Hatchery		

restaurants, shopping malls and grocery stores are available nearby, as are stops on the borough public bus system. Taxis and budget buses also offer rides. Call 255-6181 for schedule information.

The Ketchikan International Airport on Gravina Island receives jet service from points north and south. Charter and scheduled service to nearby communities is available by air taxi. Passengers and vehicles must take a small ferry from Ketchikan to Gravina Island. Ferries depart on the half-hour, with a small fee required. Taxis and airport shuttles take passengers from the airport to downtown, and several hotels offer courtesy service. Call the terminal at 225-6800 for more information.

Car rentals are available at the airport terminal. The borough bus system travels throughout most of downtown; schedules are posted at some downtown businesses.

Ketchikan has public moorage at Thomas Basin Boat Harbor, Ryus Float and City Float downtown, and at Bar Harbor a mile to the north. Contact the harbormaster between 8 a.m. and midnight on VHF Channel 16 or call 228-5637.

Accommodations

Ketchikan offers several hotels and motels, ranging from the practical to the luxurious to the historic. Numerous bed-and-breakfast establishments are open as well. Ask for the *Facilities and Attractions* brochure available from the Ketchikan Visitors Bureau.

You'll have no trouble finding a place to eat. Restaurants include Chinese, seafood, health food and fine dining.

The Ketchikan Youth Hostel, located downtown, is open in summers to travelers in the United Methodist Church, 400 Main Street, about two miles south of the ferry terminal. Write: P.O. Box 8515, Ketchikan, 99901, or call 225-3319. Late ferry arrivals are accommodated, but call first.

Recreational vehicles can park at Clover Pass Resort, 14 miles north of Ketchikan, or at Mountain Point RV Park. Check with the visitors bureau for more details. Motorhomes can park for 24 hours at the Almer Wolfe Memorial viewpoint at Mile 3.2 North Tongass Highway. A free, 24-hour dump station is located at the Public Works warehouse at 3291 Tongass Ave.

The Forest Service operates three campgrounds for a nightly fee. Signal Creek Campground, eight miles north of Ketchikan on Ward Lake, has 25 units. Last Chance Campground, with 25 units, is situated two miles beyond the Ward Lake parking lot. Three C's Campground has four spaces for backpackers and walk-ins at a site a half-mile north of Signal Creek. Check with the Forest Service or visitors bureau.

Settler's Cove is a state park recreation area with picnic tables and a dozen campsites near a sandy beach. The cove is just before the end of North Tongass Highway, at about Mile 18. Stop at the state park office at Totem Bight State Historic Park, or call 247-8574.

Excursions

Sport fishing is a major attraction in Ketchikan for visitors and residents alike. Numerous charter boats take anglers to the fishing grounds. Fishing also is featured at several lodges and wilderness resorts in the area.

Waterfront cruises offer a seaside view of Ketchikan. Those who like to boat under their own power can rent sea kayaks. Guided tours range from a few hours of paddling in Tongass Narrows or nearby coves to several days in Misty Fiords National Monument, the Barrier Islands, and elsewhere.

Several outfits offer guided tours of Ketchikan, the area's natural history and the outlying attractions. Many visit the cruise ship dock, or check at the visitors bureau.

Misty Fiords National Monument, 30 air miles east of Ketchikan, stunned its earliest white explorer, Captain George Vancouver, with its towering walls and valleys carved by glaciers. Two long fjords, stretching 117 miles and 72 miles respectively, embrace the impressive scenery, embellished with waterfalls, wildlife, and glaciers. Flightseeing trips or cruises into the wilderness area can be arranged from Ketchikan. For longer stays, take advantage of several private wilderness lodges or rent one of more than a dozen Forest Service public cabins. Despite the formidable granite walls and mountains, 15 miles of marked trails make some headway into the monument. Expect to be rained on. For more information about the monument or tour services contact the Ketchikan Ranger District or the visitors bureau.

Outdoor Recreation

As Alaska's First City, Ketchikan may as well be the first place you introduce yourself to the pleasures of exploring Alaska. Several hiking trails lead into the wilderness for those with the proper experience and equipment. The premiere view of Ketchikan is from the top of 3,000-foot Deer Mountain, reached from a three mile trail that begins at the end of Fair Street near City Park. An easier trail is the 2.5-mile Perseverance Trail, leading to Perseverance Lake. The trailhead is near Ward Lake. A mile-long trail rings Ward Lake itself. For a complete list of trails, check with the U.S. Forest Service.

11

Several lakes and coves are within reach of the road system. Ward Lake Recreation Area can be reached by way of a road that turns off at about Mile 7 North Tongass Highway. The area offers camping, hiking, picnicking, and fishing for Dolly Varden, rainbow and cutthroat trout, and salmon. Refuge Cove State Recreation Site, at about Mile 8 North Tongass Highway, is a good spot for beachcombing, picnicking and wind surfing.

Grindall Island State Marine Park, 18 air miles from Ketchikan, features a public cabin and mooring buoy in a protected cove. Reservations can be made at the State Parks Office. An overnight fee is charged.

The U.S. Forest Service maintains more than 50 public recreation cabins in the region, most requiring float plane or boat transportation to reach. An exception is Deer Mountain cabin, accessible from the Deer Mountain trail. Nightly fees and reservations are required for any cabin. Call or visit the Ketchikan Ranger District office.

Entertainment

Ketchikan's boisterous history is staged during July and August by the First City Players, who produce a musical comedy each Friday called *The Fish Pirate's Daughter* in the Main Street Theatre, 338 Main St. Call 225-4792.

Events

Some folks believe the highlight of the Blueberry Arts Festival in August is the slug races. Musical performances, a dance, arts and crafts displays and food booths fill out the entertainment. Contact the Ketchikan Area Arts and Humanities Council, Inc., at 225-2211, or write: 338 Main St., Ketchikan, 99901.

Like all of Southeast's communities, Ketchikan puts on a bang of a Fourth of July, but the Timber Carnival adds its own flair with axe-throwing, speed chopping, climbing and other lumberjack contests. Contact the Chamber of Commerce.

The annual King Salmon Derby, sponsored by the Chamber of Commerce, takes place over three weekends in late May and early June. Past winners range from a puny 44 pounds to a more respectable 79.2-pounder. Other organizations sponsor their own derbies throughout the summer.

12

Dolly's House

S tep into Dolly's House on Creek Street, and you half-expect Big Dolly herself to greet you. Simply by looking at the cracked linoleum, old-fashioned furnishings, flowery wallpaper and her best china setting the table, you wouldn't necessarily know Dolly was a sporting woman (though it's true most mature women don't have tasteful nude photographs of themselves hanging on their living room wall).

But her gaudy bedroom, with its enormous brass bed, pink bedspread, full-length mirror, lingerie and jewelry, speaks volumes about life on Creek Street—or you wish it could, anyway. Fortunately, Dolly herself gave an interview in her last years to June Allen, so much is known about both Creek Street and Dolly herself. Dolly's story is well-told in Allen's book, *Dolly's House,* but a visit to the two-story green house that preserves her belongings brings her—and Creek Street—to life.

Born in Idaho as Thelma Dolly Copeland, Dolly left her unhappy home at 13 and worked so hard at waiting tables that by the time she was in her late teens, she said, she realized she could make much more money entertaining men. After taking the career name of Dolly Arthur, she moved from the Pacific Northwest to Alaska in 1914, visiting Juneau and Petersburg before settling in Ketchikan and eventually buying No. 24 Creek Street from a fallen schoolteacher.

At 5'9" and at one time weighing as much as 240 pounds, Dolly naturally was known as Big Dolly. But she was big in spirit, too—so independent that she worked by herself, unlike most women on the street. In fact, she disliked other women, as well as most common vices. "She didn't drink or smoke, but she cussed a lot," says museum owner Laura Jackson. "She was cranky, too." Dolly wouldn't retire for the night until

13

she made $75 to $100. During prohibition, she earned even more selling illegal liquor. Guides will point out the secret cupboard and trap door she used to sneak the booze up from the creek. But, like the proverbial prostitute with a heart of gold, Dolly also gave away money, and she was sweet to most men.

Among her hobbies were cooking and her beloved exotic birds, Persian cats and pedigreed, prize-winning show dogs that wore handmade sweaters. Eventually Dolly quit cooking as her eyesight failed because she was afraid of burning herself, but you can still peruse favorite recipes like "Verifluffy Chocolate Cake" in her kitchen.

Over the years, Dolly overcame short-lived attempts to close the district (note the advertisements of Creek Street's close-out sale offering "3 glorious weeks of exotic bargains"). She also survived cancer. But she never lost her feistiness when need be, nor her business-like attitude toward money, even in retirement.

In the 1950s, when crime and other problems seemed to be getting out of hand, a grand jury investigation revealed that the chief of police ran a bawdy house. The scandal engulfed other town leaders, and in 1953 Creek Street closed.

Over the years, Dolly bought other property and houses, but No. 24 was always her home. As she grew older, her health failed, and she was forced to move to a nursing home. She died there in 1975 at the age of 86.

Dolly's House is open daily in the summer and when cruise ships are in town. A small admission is charged. A gift shop inside sells souvenirs and books. Call 225-6329.

Wrangell

Wrangell is the kind of town that doesn't beg for anyone's affections. Most people are too busy working and enjoying the great outdoors to gussy up their hometown. They like it here, so that's good enough.

If tourists are less common here than in most other Southeast communities, it's not because they're not welcome, though. In fact, the Shady Ladies, a group of women dressed up in a gold-rush version of the Welcome Wagon, meet many cruise ships and planes on behalf of the Wrangell Chamber of Commerce. After that, you're on your own, but folks are always willing to chat. Even the kids here greet strangers.

Life is simple in Wrangell. The town of 2,600 is not cluttered with traffic lights, malls or even many cars. Residents share a true sense of community here. One survey showed that over half of Wrangell's families include someone who has lived here for more than two decades, or who was even born in Alaska. In the local cafe, folks order "the usual" from waitresses who can pour on the banter as easily as they pour out the coffee. People like jawing with their neighbors here. When residents were asked several years ago if they would prefer home postal delivery to picking up their mail at the post office, they said no. They didn't want to surrender the daily ritual of getting the mail and visiting with friends.

If Wrangell's charms seem modest to those expecting another tourist town, its outdoor attractions border on the spectacular. Several miles north of Wrangell, the Stikine River emerges from a 400-mile journey from Canada to provide a vast playground where people can cross the river flats, soak in hot springs, hunt, camp, and ogle everything from a miniature grand canyon to a gold rush town. LeConte Glacier, a nearby black bear observatory, and good fishing and hunting complete the equation.

Much of Wrangell's livelihood revolves around the harbor, which is protected by a curlicue of land. Fishing and fish processing are major industries. (A bumper sticker spotted on a Wrangell pickup truck: "Have you flogged your crew today?") Processors put up salmon, halibut, black cod, bottom fish, shrimp and dungeness crab, and many fishermen sell their catches on the docks. One sign of spring is when a civic-minded fisherman gives away herring roe—considered a delicacy—at the docks to townspeople.

The town's other lifeblood is the Alaska Pulp Company sawmill, about six miles south of town on Zimovia Highway. The sawmill is the town's largest employer, with a payroll of about 180 people. Most of the 250,000 board feet processed here daily (that's enough for 20 average homes) is harvested from the Tongass National Forest and destined for Japanese markets. You may see one of the giant ocean-going freighters headed for the mill dock.

"It's a dirty little town, but we like it that way," a mayor once joked. Dirty, no. Tough, yes. Wrangell has survived the kind of ups and downs that would have sunk a less hardy bunch. For more than a century, the community has weathered various booms and busts brought on by furs, gold, fish, and timber.

Modern Wrangell seems so unassuming it may be difficult to imagine that this spot has been coveted since Alaska's earliest times, when un-known people left behind mysterious stone carvings near the island's tip. The area's complex past is due to the intersection of history formed by the mighty Stikine River and the Inside Passage. Over the centuries, the town site passed through the dominion of the Stikine Tlingits into the hands of the British, Russians and Americans. In fact, the town likes to advertise itself as being the only Alaska community having existed under the rule of three flags (really three forts) and four nations. Today a visitor can find traces from all of Wrangell's occupiers.

After the fur trade dwindled, three different gold strikes in Canada stirred Wrangell up between 1860 and 1898, but by the turn of the century, the town depended on the same industries that sustain it today—fishing, canneries, and a sawmill that was probably the first in the territory and was the first to hire women in 1929. Major fires in 1906 and 1952 tested the community's resilience, but people always rebuilt. When the town's major fish processor and the sawmill closed for a time in the mid-1980s, the community hung on until the businesses re-opened.

In recent years, the town's history has come full circle as Wrangell serves as a base for mineral exploration in British Columbia. A Canadian mine company, Cominco, now transports gold concentrate by Hovercraft down the 60 miles down Stikine River to Wrangell, where it is shipped to other ports and Japanese refineries.

Today, many of Wrangell's strongest ties to the past remain constant—in the area's natural beauty, the names plucked from history, the proud Native culture, and, of course, the ever-flowing Stikine River.

Attractions

No need for tour buses in Wrangell. The downtown area is laid out along the waterfront and circles the town's bustling harbor. An afternoon's stroll takes you past most of the major sights and through the town's layers of history.

One of the area's attractions will likely come to you. Wrangell children meet nearly every daytime ferry or cruise ship to sell garnets chipped from a ledge near the mouth of the Stikine River. Only the town's youngsters are allowed to sell the stones without a permit.

Ferry passengers in port for just an hour or so have time to wander to Petroglyph Beach, about 3/4 mile north of the terminal. Along the way you'll pass Our Collections Museum, a private collection. Wrangell's petroglyphs are a perpetual reminder that enigmas still exist in Alaska. No one really knows whether the strange shapes signify territorial markers, supplications, forerunners of totemic designs, or simply doodles made by the region's earliest residents.

Low tide is the best viewing time. Head north on Evergreen Avenue, which parallels the beach. Signs direct the way down a dirt road to a boardwalk. At the beach, turn right and walk to the large rock outcropping above the high tide line. Search in the jumble of rock for the carvings, most of which face seaward. You'll feel a sense of discovery as you locate the mysterious spirals, circles, fish and other shapes pecked into the rocks.

17

When ships arrive in port, the children of Wrangell open shop and sell locally gathered garnets to visitors.

Many visitors like to make stone rubbings with paper and wax or fern leaves. Wrangell gift stores sell supplies. Locals advise that photographs are most successful when the rocks are wet and when the evening or afternoon light from the west provides contrast.

If you don't have time to visit the beach, you can see a few petroglyphs and rubbings at the Wrangell Museum on Second Street. The collection is a good introduction to the area's sweep of history. Operated by the Wrangell Historical Society, the non-profit museum is tucked into the town's first modern schoolhouse, built in 1906 and now on the National Register of Historic Sites. The museum is open for summer visitors Monday through Saturday from 1 p.m. to 4 p.m., or when cruise ships or ferries are in town for at least one hour. There is a small admission fee. Call 874-3770 for information.

Inside you'll find a homey atmosphere with old-fashioned cases displaying many items and photographs from Wrangell's past. Exhibit rooms feature natural history mounts, Native artifacts and tools, fishing and logging exhibits, early newspaper equipment from the *Wrangell Sentinel*, and antiques from local businesses. Don't miss the dented metal bucket with bullet-sized tooth holes made by a determined bear.

Among the museum's treasures are four ancient house posts of the tribal house of Chief Shakes, the most influential clan leader of the Stikines. Oral tradition says that more than a thousand years ago, the Stikine Tlingit, or Shtax'heen Kwan, established villages along the lower part of the river and on nearby islands. Like the white traders and settlers who followed them, the Stikines thrived on the region's fish, game, furs, berries and trade routes. A group settled the village of Kotzlitzna, or Old Town, about 18 miles south of present-day Wrangell.

In 1834 the Russian-American Company bought land from the Tlingits at the edge of the harbor and built a Russian outpost, Redoubt St. Dionysius, to keep rival British traders of the Hudson's Bay Company from moving in on "their" territory. About 1,500 Tlingits moved outside the fort, both to take advantage of trade opportunities and to keep their eyes on the interlopers.

Six years later, the British leased a large tract of trading territory and the Russian fort, which they renamed Fort Stikine. They spent much of their time dealing with the contentious Natives. The British were not tenants for long after the fur market declined. In 1870, three years after the

American flag rose over Alaska, the U.S. Army built its own outpost, named Fort Wrangell after Baron Ferdinand von Wrangell, chief manager of the Russian-American Company from 1830-36. The cornerstone of the American fort is displayed in the museum courtyard.

The U.S. Post Office and Customs House, a stolid building on Front Street a block below the museum, was built in 1940-41 on the former site of Fort Wrangell. The fort's cornerstone turned up during its construction. Several important people in Alaska and Wrangell history served as postmasters, including the missionary S. Hall Young.

Young's influence can also be seen on Church Street, so named for the several churches gracing the lane. The First Presbyterian Church was founded in 1879 by Young. The church's mission began with Mrs. Amanda McFarland, who had arrived two years previously. Mrs. McFarland opened a school for girls located where the high school is today. A fire claimed the original church in 1930 and damaged its replacement again in 1978. The red neon cross rising over the town was added in 1939 and is listed as an official navigational aid on nautical charts. "The crews of many storm-tossed ships have expressed gratitude for the availability of the cross light," says the church's historical marker.

Also established at about the same time was First Presbyterian's neighbor, St. Rose of Lima Catholic Church, a lovely white building decorated with a striking rose stained-glass window above the door. Just down the street, at the intersection of Episcopal Avenue and Church Street, is St. Phillip's Episcopal Church. Wrangell Natives donated land and built the church in 1903, originally calling it the People's Church of Wrangell. Several other churches are located on nearby streets.

A small park on Episcopal Avenue and Front Street reflects the Natives' pride in their past. A group of four poles marks the site of the original Sun House and the first Kiksadi totem raised in 1895 to honor Chief Kahlteen, leader of the Wrangell Kiksadi clan. A replica of this pole and other important totems stand here now.

Other interesting totems are located at City Hall, the Irene Ingle Public Library, the Wrangell City Museum and the U.S. Post Office. The reproductions often were made by local carvers, some employed by the Civilian Conservation Corps in the 1930s and 1940s. The Wrangell Indian Association, the Sealaska Corporation, business people and civic organizations all

20

have contributed to the revival of local Native culture.

The most important tribute to Wrangell's original residents is the Chief Shakes tribal house, on Shakes Island. Walk along Shakes Street toward the harbor; signs mark the way to the footbridge crossing the harbor to the park. The present tribal house is a scaled-down replica of the original Shakes clan house. The Russian fort of St. Dionysius, and later the British Fort Stikine, were located at the harbor's edge, where the Hungry Beaver Restaurant and Marine Bar are today.

The name Shakes was a derivation of the original "We-Shakes," which represented the sound a killer whale's tail makes splashing the water. The name belonged to a bested chief of the Niska tribe, who awarded his killer whale hat and the title "We-Shakes" to the victor, now known as Shakes I. His descendant, Shakes V, dealt with the Russians, and later the British and Americans.

During this era, the Natives' cultural integrity crumbled under the influence of government and missionaries. Natives moved into individual homes, were discouraged from speaking their tongue in school, attended church and changed their funeral customs. Instead of being cremated, for example, Shakes V was buried in a grave surrounded by a Russian-style picket fence. The grave lies at Case Street, across the harbor from the island. When Shakes VI died in 1916, he was given a Christian burial in the town cemetery.

In the late 1930s, President Franklin Roosevelt's Civilian Conservation Corps took on the Totem Restoration Project. The community house itself was built in three years, with workers earning $2 per day. They used wooden pegs and tools of the original style to construct the building and work the spruce planks. In 1940, Charlie Jones, also called Kudanake, was inducted as Chief Shakes VII at an enormous potlatch at the clan house attended by thousands of people, including Native leaders and representatives of Alaska and the United States and Canadian governments. Chief Shakes VII was the last to assume the title.

Built in the traditional manner, the house has three levels, where the 80 or so family members and additional slaves cooked, lived and slept. The chief's private area was behind the wall screen, which today is painted with a design from one of his Chilkat blankets. The four house posts are colorful replicas of the originals brought from Old Town and now displayed at the

Totem poles fill the yard at Chief Shakes house.

Wrangell Museum. When the original house was built, 100 slaves were sacrificed for each house post as a sign of Shakes' wealth and status.

Today, visitors to the house can see photos of the construction process and potlatch, a picture of Chief Shakes VI lying in state, and other interesting artifacts, including a pair of mud skis used for traveling the Stikine River mud flats. The set of killer whale posts displayed inside once guarded Chief Shakes V's grave.

Most poles surrounding the clan house are replicas of important poles belonging to Chief Shakes and to Chief Kadashan, remembered as a great orator and peacemaker, among other accomplishments. Kadashan's tribal house was located across the harbor from the island. A favorite totem with visitors is the whimsical Three Frogs Totem, originally created as a ridicule pole to shame debtors into paying. The replicated pole, which is badly decaying, has been taken down with plans for eventual copying.

The house is open when cruise ships are in town, or by appointment with the Wrangell Museum. Stop by the museum or call 874-3770. The museum also sells a booklet written by E.L. Keithahn, *The Authentic History of Shakes Island and Clan*, which contains an exciting account of the war between the Niskas and Stikines, as well as the history of the chiefs

22

and the Shakes House.

Wrangell's Front Street, where most merchants do business, still retains a frontier feel thanks to the remaining false-fronted historic buildings that survived major fires and other calamities over the years. Plaques installed on most of the town's significant buildings outline the colorful past and progression of owners of these otherwise simple structures.

A few empty buildings still retain the hollow-eyed look reminiscent of abandoned gold towns. Three Canadian gold rushes boosted Wrangell's fortunes because of its location as a supply center at the mouth of the Stikine, which served as a kind of highway into the gold fields. The first rush in 1861 fizzled quickly, but the 1872 Cassiar strike attracted more than a thousand miners. "They turned the old fur-trading post into a metropolis of riotous sport, and prosperity reigned," wrote historian C.L. Andrews. "Gamblers and ladies of leisure came from Victoria, the roulette wheels whirled and the dance-halls flourished."

During the Klondike rush of 1898, nearly 5,000 miners flooded Wrangell believing the Stikine would offer easy passage to the gold fields. After the Canadians reneged on a promise to build a railroad from the river to the Klondike, prospectors wised up and attempted other routes.

The *Wrangell Sentinel* building, 312 Front St., is worth noting because the newspaper's history exemplifies the town's hardy nature. The *Sentinel's* masthead reads "Oldest Continuously Published Newspaper in Alaska," no small feat in a territory where newspapers bloomed and died in gold camps and towns as quickly as dandelions. (The *Sentinel* was not, however, the first paper in Alaska or Wrangell.) The paper was founded in 1902, the same year the town's name changed from Fort Wrangell to Wrangell. When the building burned in 1906, the *Sentinel's* publishers used butcher paper and red paint to put out a makeshift paper. A 1952 fire that razed half of the town's businesses spared the *Sentinel*, but the publishers were forced to work amid household belongings stored by the homeless while they again rebuilt.

Visitor Information

Wrangell Visitors Center is located in an A-frame cabin on Outer Drive, adjacent to City Hall and near the waterfront. Look for the tall totem

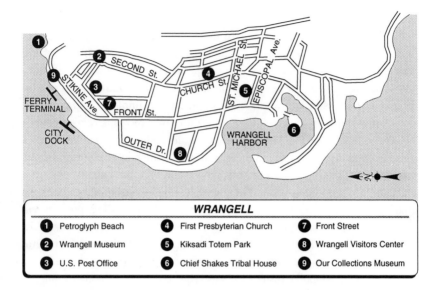

WRANGELL

① Petroglyph Beach   ④ First Presbyterian Church   ⑦ Front Street

② Wrangell Museum   ⑤ Kiksadi Totem Park   ⑧ Wrangell Visitors Center

③ U.S. Post Office   ⑥ Chief Shakes Tribal House   ⑨ Our Collections Museum

pole. The center is open when cruise ships and ferries are in town, and during other hours. Write: Wrangell Chamber of Commerce, Box 49V, Wrangell, 99929. Call 874-3901.

U.S. Forest Service Wrangell Ranger District office is open during working hours at 525 Bennett St., about a mile from the ferry terminal. Write to: P.O. Box 51, Wrangell, 99929. Call 874-2323. Rangers sometimes meet ferries on weekends with information.

The *Wrangell Sentinel* distributes the *Wrangell Guide*, a free publication detailing local attractions and services. Write: P.O. Box 798, Wrangell, 99929, or call 874-2301. The newspaper office is at 312 Front St.

Transportation

Wrangell Airport is served by charter air services and daily jet flights. The airport is about a mile from downtown. A rental car agency and taxi service are available in town. The state ferry docks at a terminal on Stikine Avenue, a few blocks from downtown. Call 874-3711 for 24-hour recorded information about departures and arrivals. Cruise ships moor at the city dock downtown.

Excursions

The Stikine River entices visitors who want to explore a world different from the maritime character of the Inside Passage. Mountains, gorges, glaciers and a wide variety of wildlife accompany the Stikine on its wild journey through Canada and Alaska. Charter boats are available in Wrangell for day trips up the river to explore the Wrangell Garnet Ledge, sloughs, waterfalls, and Shakes Glacier. Time permitting, some trips venture as far as the U.S.-Canadian border. About 200 miles upstream is the river's own Grand Canyon, a rift 55 miles long with walls as high as 1,000 feet. Telegraph Creek, once a gold rush town, is located at the canyon's west end.

Chief Shakes Hot Springs is located about 12 miles up the Stikine River on a slough. The water temperature is a delicious 122 degrees F. The spring features enclosed and open-air tubs, a dressing room, tables and outhouse, but no overnight accommodations. A Forest Service cabin is located nearby.

Petersburg residents feel proprietary about LeConte Glacier, but the tidewater glacier is only 25 miles north of Wrangell and is easily accessible by plane or boat.

The Anan Bear Observatory brings people and black bears within safe viewing distance at Anan Creek on the mainland, about 31 miles from Wrangell by boat or 50 minutes by air. The bears arrive in July and August to fatten up on the pink salmon run. Seals and eagles turn up on the chow line as well. The observation deck overlooks a waterfall. Those who wish to stay overnight can reserve use of a Forest Service cabin located about a mile from the observatory. (Note: The trail between the cabin and creek is used by bears, too.)

The agency recently conducted a three-year survey of human and bear interactions to help determine whether the observatory is growing too popular with visitors. In 1991, 1,500 people traveled to the creek. Check with the Forest Service Wrangell District Office to see if permits are required or to register for the cabin. If you're not experienced in bear country, take time to learn proper behavior at the observatory. Information about boat or air charter services is available at the visitor information center.

Outdoor recreation

Those who would like to spend a few nights enjoying the real Alaska have a choice of over 20 public Forest Service cabins scattered throughout the bays, islands, lakes, and forest near Wrangell. Most are accessible only by float plane or boat. Permits are required and can be obtained in person or by mail from Wrangell Ranger District. A nightly fee is charged. For information about specific cabins, contact the office. The Forest Service office also sells the *Wrangell Island Road Guide*, valuable for exploring trails, scenic overlooks, picnic areas, beaches and lakes. Also available are maps detailing canoe and kayak routes on the Stikine River.

Easy hiking treks include Rainbow Falls Trail, which takes less than a mile to climb from Shoemaker Bay harbor parking lot to observation points overlooking Rainbow Falls. A trail up Mount Dewey, behind the town, allows you to walk in John Muir's footsteps. The hike begins from Third Street. Ask the Forest Service for its brochure listing other trails.

Much of Wrangell Island is seamed with one-lane, gravel logging roads. Though open to public travel, these roads are best-suited to the adventurous. There are no guard rails or shoulders, and logging trucks have the right-of-way (as if there were any question of it). Given all these precautions, drivers will find that the roads penetrate to some of Wrangell's most scenic spots. Take along the Forest Service road guide.

Accommodations

Wrangell has a few motels, lodges and bed-and-breakfast establishments located downtown or close to it. Since the choice is limited, it can't hurt to ask a local for recommendations or to check the hostelries out before handing over your money.

Eateries are similarly limited, but you can choose from among pizza, deli fare, cafe staples and hotel restaurants. Ask a resident for advice.

Recreational vehicles and tent campers can stay at the Shoemaker Bay Recreation Area at Mile 4.6 Zimovia Highway. Operated by the City of Wrangell, the park features a boat harbor, RV parking, a boat launch, and tent camping. Services include water, a dump site, playground equipment, a tennis court, a picnic shelter and a rest room. Reservations can be made at City Hall at 874-2381.

Tent camping for one night only is available at City Park, one mile south of Wrangell on Zimovia Highway. Park facilities include picnic tables, shelters and rest rooms.

The Overlook Observation Point, about 22 miles from Wrangell, offers unimproved RV camping in an abandoned rock pit. Note that this spot is reached by a single-lane gravel road.

A dump site and water are available downtown near the corner of Front Street and Case Avenue. Look for an orange door in the ground.

Pats Lake campground, about 11 miles south of Wrangell, is a largely unimproved area with places for vehicles and tents. For more information and directions, contact the Wrangell Chamber of Commerce, which runs the campground with the Girl Scouts and Lions Club. A fee is charged at the site. Fishing, canoeing, and hiking are possible at the lake.

Our Collections Museum

Some people say Elva Bigelow's private museum is a hodgepodge. One tour guide calls it a "garage sale waiting to happen." Mrs. Bigelow just laughs when she hears that. She thinks of it a little differently. "It's our family things. Our collections," she says. "That's why I named it that way."

Our Collections Museum is literally a gathering of items that Mrs. Bigelow and her late husband, Bolly, used, enjoyed and collected over a half-century. Some might relegate such artifacts to either the attic or the trash bin, but Mrs. Bigelow displays hers in a large warehouse next to her waterfront home on Evergreen Avenue. "See, I don't patronize the dump too much," she says. "Before, I had so many things in boxes. Then I thought of this idea."

Dominating the cavernous room is a 20-foot long plaster model of Wrangell that shows the town's layout in miniature but faithful detail. With friends, she and her husband built the diorama in honor of Alaska's centennial in 1967. Crowded around the display are hundreds of interesting items arranged in glass cases, dangling from rafters and hanging on walls. Many are relics from a life spent in Alaska: snowshoes; fish nets; mink, marten and bear traps; several antique outboard motor engines; a pair of broad, hand-made wooden skis with leather traps. Mrs. Bigelow points out an old-fashioned backpack crafted from a wood frame and laced-up canvas. "It's brought out lots of moose meat," she says. A blonde wolverine skin and thick black bear skin draw the attention of many visitors, while hunters like to eye the ranks of rifles hanging on a wall. "Those rifles earned their retirement," she says.

The museum gives many older visitors a chance to stroll down memory lane, when everyday tasks weren't so simple. Washboards, wringers and tubs, a blacksmith forge and anvil, a cracked horse collar, ancient typewriters, radios and sewing machines—all evoke times past. Some are irresistible to visitors. Mrs. Bigelow points out a hand-cranked fog horn from a sailing ship. She had to disconnect the bells. "You know these little boys 25 and older—they like to play with them and it just echoes in here," she says.

Mrs. Bigelow also offers her own hand-made crafts for sale, including crocheted doll clothes, Christmas tree skirts and scarves. Each morning she spends a couple of hours gathering examples of Southeast Alaska plants and flowers to display in the museum for the edification and enjoyment of visitors.

Today, Mrs. Bigelow regrets she didn't store even more belongings over the years. "If I had any idea that I would have opened something like this, I would have saved things from territorial times," she says.

Several thousand visitors stop by Our Collections Museum each season, she estimates. Not everyone is interested in her lifetime of belongings, but some covet certain pieces for themselves. No such luck. "They're just not for sale," she says firmly. "If I just sold one item at a time, I wouldn't have anything left."

Our Collections Museum is a brief walk from the ferry terminal and downtown Wrangell. The museum, on the beach side of Evergreen Avenue, is marked by signs. Admission is by donation. Hours are when cruise ships and ferries are in port, or by appointment. Call 874-3646.

Petersburg

The best approach to Petersburg is by sea, for this is a town founded and peopled by those who make their living from the ocean's harvest. From the water, you see how firmly the community embraces its livelihood. The town curves around the waterfront, where three harbors thrive on the labors of fishermen and cannery workers, and piers and wharves extend long fingers into Wrangell Narrows. Fishing is a year-round proposition here, as fleets pursue halibut and herring in the spring, salmon in the summer, crab in the winter, and shrimp all the year.

Petersburg is about as pretty as fishing towns come, framed by the waters of Frederick Sound and Wrangell Narrows, and punctuated by Devil's Thumb, a spire that marks the Canadian border in the distance. In the yards of the neat bungalow homes, crab pots pile up and fishermen sit patiently mending their nets. The Petersburg High School Class of '95 advertises that it will clean herring boats to raise money for a trip to Europe. The local bookstore sells commercial fishing licenses. The 24-hour Homestead Cafe offers 24 hours of fishing gossip.

Here you'll encounter more residents than fellow visitors. (The residents are the ones asking how you're enjoying your visit.) Only the state ferries and the smallest of cruise ships can maneuver through the Wrangell Narrows, a skinny channel not even 30 feet deep that separates Petersburg's Mitkof Island from Kupreanof Island. Thus, Petersburg's 3,600 residents keep largely to themselves. Store windows are more likely to display pottery by high school art students or the names of babies born that week than tourist trinkets. "It's a family town, not a tourist town," said resident Troy Blatchford in *No Show Tonight*, a town history. "But we still say 'Velkommen til Petersburg.' "

31

At no time is that welcome extended so heartily as during the town's annual Little Norway Festival, which takes place each year on the weekend closest to Norway's Independence Day, May 17. Visitors quickly learn that nobody eats, drinks, dances and makes merry like those Norwegians—or honorary Norwegians. The revelry not only celebrates the official holiday, but Petersburg's roots. Unlike any other community in Southeast Alaska, Petersburg's heritage is largely Scandinavian. Many families are fourth- and fifth-generation descendants of immigrant fishermen who came here seeking the sea-going livelihood they could no longer find in their own country's waters.

It was such a man who founded Petersburg and lent it his name. Local lore says Norwegian Peter Buschmann chose this spot in 1897 for a cannery because of good timber, rich fishing grounds, and mountains and fjords that reminded him of his native country. Whatever the reasons, the original cannery operation soon expanded into a sawmill, warehouses and bunkhouses for whites and Chinese laborers. From the very start, Petersburg became known for its halibut. Norwegian immigrants flocked to the growing community to fish, followed by friends and family.

Fishing was a tough proposition then, even though halibut, black cod, salmon and herring were plentiful. Boats, most built in Petersburg, were powered by oars or sails until about World War II. Young boys began fishing with the men of the family as young as 12. Despite weeks of backbreaking work in often terrible weather, the catches sometimes brought little pay. During the Depression, for example, some fishermen found their halibut sold for only 1 to 1.5 cents per pound. Some old salts remember lassoing icebergs in Frederick Sound to break up and pack fish in.

When Petersburg later proved to be poised on rich shrimp grounds, canny businessmen took advantage of this boon to pioneer the territory's first shrimp cannery. Clams and crab have also been processed over the decades. Modern innovations streamlined the work, but cannery workers still flock to town each summer to work packing and processing, and the fishy aroma still drifts over town. Eventually, timber became a lesser light in the town's economy.

For many years, Norwegian was commonly spoken on the streets and in stores. In school, kids cussed in their native tongue. The town bound itself into a close-knit—some said clannish—community. Women and

The ferry *Matanuska* prepares to unload cars near downtown Petersburg.

older children, then as now, often worked in the canneries putting up the pack, as did Tlingit, Chinese and Filipino workers. Older residents claim women ran the town because the men fished so much. (Some say that's still true.) In 1910 the town was incorporated, and a city council took charge of local government. Neat white homes, plank roads and stores crept from the waterfront onto the soggy muskeg and along the shores.

A town with a thousand bachelor fishermen had certain business needs, encouraging the establishment of once boisterous saloons like Jim Brennan's Bucket of Blood, located where the post office stands today. Nearby was the red light district, home to bordellos operated by such women as Black Mary. During the day, old-timers say, the prostitutes looked no different than other woman, except they were better dressed.

This was a family town, too, so plenty of legitimate entertainment existed at the movie house, roller rink, ice cream parlor and card room. Dancing at the Sons of Norway Hall gave all those bachelor fishermen the chance to flirt with local beauties. Hunting and fishing were popular pastimes, though they provided more dinner than sport.

Today, Norwegian is no longer a common language, but the community fosters small touches of the old world. Rosemaling, a delicate and colorful style of folk painting, accents many storefronts. The local bakery sells krumkaker and other Scandinavian delicacies. Gift shops offer more Norwegian souvenirs than Alaskan (a favorite bumper sticker jokes about a certain fish dish of ill-repute: "When lutefisk is outlawed, only outlaws will have lutefisk").

Though the population is no longer distilled Norwegian, scan the phone book and you'll see names from the town's earliest days: Buschmann, Ohmer, Lee, Enge, Otness. Many children join their fathers and mothers at sea when they're of age. Petersburg's history is still walking around the streets.

Attractions

Entering the town proper of Petersburg, it's impossible to resist photographing the Sons of Norway Hall or the picturesque homes reflected in Hammer Slough. Taking pictures of the slough is practically mandatory, in fact. The white hall, brightened with flowery vines of rosemaling on the shutters, was built in 1912 and is now on the National Register of Historic Places. In the old days, the stately building was the center of activities for the fraternal organization and often rang with music as townspeople gathered for Saturday night dances. Today the hall is used for wedding receptions, bingo, and community events. Upstairs a gift and craft shop, Husfliden, sells Norwegian and Alaskan items Mondays through Saturdays during the summer.

Next to the Sons of Norway Hall is the Viking ship *Valhalla*. The 30-foot vessel was constructed in 1976 by a New Jersey shipwright in honor of the nation's bicentennial and eventually passed into the hands of the Sons of Norway for the bargain-basement price of $1. Portrayed on the sail is a two-headed raven, a symbol for the Norse god Odin. An earlier version of the ship was once spirited away to Wrangell by pranksters.

Sing Lee Alley, a side street to Nordic Drive, evokes Petersburg's early days with its false-front buildings. The street is named for a well-liked dry goods merchant, Sing Lee, who is still remembered by many old-timers for his generosity in distributing candy to children, supplies to the needy, and loans to miners and fishermen. Sing Lee arrived in 1909 and opened his store where Kito's Kave is located today. One of Petersburg's mysteries is the unsolved murder of Sing Lee in 1932, though old-timers say the federal marshal was responsible.

The Clausen Memorial Museum, at 203 Fram Street, is another legacy of Alaska's Centennial celebration. Built in 1967, the museum is a time capsule of Petersburg's history, maritime and otherwise. "Everybody around here has a favorite area," a museum volunteer says. That's probably because their families donated photographs, furniture, jewelry and other personal items to the museum.

If you doubt that Petersburg is a fishing capital, wander through the museum's displays of fishing techniques and handmade wooden gear, such as a rudimentary fish finder. Sure to impress sport anglers is a photograph of what appears to be a barn door but is actually a 344-pound halibut caught at nearby Thomas Bay in 1986. Even more impressive is the mount of the world record king salmon, an estimated 126.5 pounds. Caught in 1939 in a fish trap near Prince of Wales Island, the fish was described by the crew of the boat that brought it in as "thick as a pig." Putting up the salmon's meat required 104 canning jars.

The museum is open weekdays during the summer in the afternoons and on Tuesday mornings. A small admission is required. Call 772-3598.

The heart of Petersburg is in the harbors. The town's commercial and pleasure fleets fill three harbors prosaically named North, Middle and South. Benches and picnic tables overlook North Harbor (that's the one at far right as you face the waterfront). For anyone who loves the sea or its servants, few things could be more pleasurable than strolling along these docks and admiring the boats. From the deep-chested tugs to the old, wooden trollers, the fleets evoke the lore of the sea. At the proper seasons, you may see deck hands baiting the large hooks of the long-lines for Alaska's hectic 24-hour halibut openings, fishermen mending salmon nets, or crews scrubbing down boats after unloading a hold full of herring. Looking at the faces of today's fishermen, it's not hard to imagine some of the men who bore such nicknames as Black Cod Eric, Jump Spark, Two-by-Four John, Laughing Swede, and Atomic Ole.

Just past the downtown stores and across from the Petersburg Fisheries, Inc., complex rests a boulder marking the spot of Peter Buschmann's cannery, which led to PFI. Another local landmark, Eagle's Roost Park, can be found farther down Nordic Drive, just beyond the cannery plant. Here wives once gathered to look for their husbands returning from the fishing grounds. With benches and flowers, this grassy oasis is ideal for spotting eagles, which often hang out in the surrounding spruce trees. A nearby staircase leads to the beach, where you may see young anglers casting for Dolly Varden, gardeners gathering seaweed for fertilizer, tug-boats towing log rafts, and boats of all kinds entering or leaving Wrangell Narrows.

Across the channel is Kupreanof Island, where fox farmers once ranched furs and dairy cows once grazed on rich estuary grass. The houses sprin-kling the island's shore represent the City of Kupreanof, populated by about 50 extremely independent and sometimes ornery Alaskans. Local radio personality and periodic mayor of Kupreanof Harold Bergmann once wrote that the town has "no nothin" and that's the way they like it. The *Kupreanof News*, a monthly newsletter, reveals the community's casual approach to government. When a resident interested in joining the city council was quizzed about his opinions of the town's founding philosophy, "Mayor [Sharon] Sprague liked what she heard and appointed Herb to fill the vacant seat," the newsletter reported. Although Kupreanof's residents value their privacy, they join forces to oppose any groups trying to foist progress on them.

Many of Petersburg's attractions lie along the Mitkof Highway, which stretches about 34 miles to the south end of the island. The first 18 miles are paved. Logging roads extend from the highway across the island's expanse to remote lakes, creeks and coves. Ask for a road map at the visitor information center.

In late summer or early fall, stop at the Falls Creek fish ladder at Mile 10.8 Mitkof Highway for views of spawning pink and silver salmon. At Mile 11, turn right toward Papke's Landing, once the home of one of Petersburg's most charming and eccentric characters, Herman Papke. From 1902 to his death in 1964, he kept a remarkable diary of his life in his little cabin here. Legend says he's the one who spread lupine flowers around the island. Whether that's true or not, he was known for his exceptional gardens and apple trees. He even grew tobacco.

His cabin was crammed with stuff ranging from bird skulls to empty tin cans, as if he never threw anything away. He wore his gray wool underwear all winter long and was known to raise his bread dough by bringing it into his bunk. For a long time he feuded with Charles Elliott, a Scotsman who lived across the Narrows on Kupreanof Island. Papke was not a hermit, though, and he delighted in visitors. In 1935 the community forged a road out to his property and built a dock. When his cabin burned, the townspeople built him another one. Papke helped them by phoning the switchboard when steamers passed through the Narrows so townspeople would be ready to greet the boat.

Today wild raspberries and strawberries still grow at the landing, but if you visit you're more likely to see log rafts and fishing boats. Transient boat moorage is available here.

See the section on outdoor recreation for more attractions along the Mitkof Highway.

Visitor Information

The Petersburg Chamber of Commerce runs a visitor information center at 1st and Fram streets in conjunction with the U.S. Forest Service. Area maps, brochures and other information are available. Ask for the list of services and attractions. Write: Box 649, Petersburg, 99833. Call 772-3646.

The Forest Service's Petersburg Ranger District office is on the second floor of the U.S. Post Office building on Nordic Drive. Call 772-3871 or write: P.O. Box 1328, Petersburg, 99833.

The free *Viking Visitor Guide* is published by the *Petersburg Pilot* and is distributed throughout town. The newspaper office is at 212 Harbor Way, across from North Harbor, or write: P.O. Box 930, Petersburg, 99833. Call 772-9393.

Transportation

Like most communities in Southeast, you can't drive to Petersburg. Daily jet flights connect Petersburg with Juneau and Seattle. Small plane services commute between neighboring communities or offer charters to remote sites. The airport is about a mile east from town.

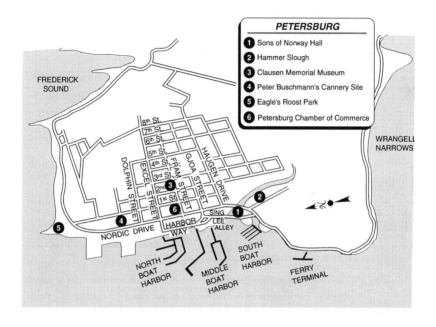

PETERSBURG

1 Sons of Norway Hall
2 Hammer Slough
3 Clausen Memorial Museum
4 Peter Buschmann's Cannery Site
5 Eagle's Roost Park
6 Petersburg Chamber of Commerce

State ferries dock at a terminal about one mile south of town. Only small cruise ships can travel the shallow waters of Wrangell Narrows. Stretching 21 miles between Mitkof and Kupreanof islands, the channel averages but a half-mile in width. You'll feel like sucking in your stomach when the ferry squeezes through the skinniest part, just 100 yards wide. The passage has been dredged twice, but in some spots it is so shallow that a low tide forces the ferry to delay. More than 70 buoys and markers mark the sea lane, so that at night it twinkles with red and green lights like a Christmas tree (which is what most people compare it with).

Rental cars are available from the larger motels and at the airport. Taxi service is available at the airport and ferry terminal.

Transient moorage is available at North Harbor. Check with the harbormaster's office before docking by radioing on VHF Channel 16, CB Channel 9, or by calling 772-4688. The office is located above North Harbor.

Accommodations

Petersburg has four inns and a couple of bed-and-breakfast homes. You should have no trouble picking a place, as they offer a variety of services ranging from kitchenettes, scenic views, proximity to the ferry terminal, and bike, car, and boat rentals. Ask at the visitor center for a list of services.

Recreational vehicle parks are located in town and on the highway. A staging area between the ferry terminal and town allows RVs to park overnight only. LeConte RV Park on Haugen Drive downtown has spaces and other services. Twin Creek RV Park is at Mile 7 Mitkof Highway and also has standard services. Sumner Strait Campground, at the end of a narrow road leading from 26 Mile Mitkof Highway, has no facilities.

Camping could be difficult for those on foot. The City of Petersburg runs Tent City about 1.5 miles from downtown in a muskeg meadow, but the platforms are generally occupied by cannery workers and the site is not recommended for families. More information is available at the city offices, across from the U.S. Post Office on Nordic Drive, or call 772-4425.

Ohmer Creek Campground at Mile 22 Mitkof Highway has room for tents or RVs, tables, grills and rest rooms.

Restaurants are varied with Chinese-American fare, health food, seafood, pizza, fine dining, and diner meals available.

Excursions

Some people come to Petersburg for nothing more than the fishing. Numerous charters are happy to oblige with salmon and halibut fishing packages. Fly-in freshwater fishing trips are popular, too. Local businesses will smoke or can your catches. You can also buy processed fish if you come back empty-handed.

Those more interested in sightseeing will appreciate nearby LeConte Glacier, the southernmost tidewater glacier on the continent. The glacier calves almost constantly. Marine wildlife is a bonus. Tours include flightseeing by helicopter or small plane, sea kayaking, and charter cruises.

The Stikine River delta fans out near the south end of Mitkof Island. Jet boat tours up the river, or rafting/paddling excursions down river are based in Petersburg.

39

Short harbor tours cruise the busy waterfront, and whale watching and photographic expeditions in Frederick Sound and elsewhere can also be arranged. Some establishments rent skiffs and gear. Several outlying lodges can be reached from Petersburg. Local guides provide tours of town, the shrimp cannery, and the island. Ask for the list of charter and guide services from the visitor center to pare your choices.

Outdoor Recreation

Sandy Beach Picnic Area is but a mile from downtown Petersburg. Shelters, stone fireplaces, running water and great views of Frederick Sound make this popular with residents.

Fishermen will enjoy Blind River Rapids at Mile 14.5 Mitkof Highway. A short boardwalk across the muskeg leads to a near-idyllic vista of the shallow river and estuary. Hatchery steelhead, king salmon, coho, Dolly Varden and cutthroat challenge anglers during different seasons.

Winter visitors should stop at Mile 16 Mitkof, where a blind allows views of wintering trumpeter swans on Blind Slough.

Blind Slough Recreation Area at Mile 17 has picnic shelters, outhouses and peaceful views of the grassy estuary and hovering mountains. Crystal Lake Fish Hatchery is across the slough.

Trails on Mitkof and Kupreanof islands suit hikers of all abilities. The Frederick Point Boardwalk crosses muskeg and a salmon stream with a mile-long stretch of planks. The trail begins next to Sandy Beach Recreation Area. Raven Trail is a challenging hike beginning behind the Petersburg Airport and heading uphill for views of Petersburg and surrounding waters. You'll need a boat to reach Kupreanof Island trails to the top of Petersburg Mountain or along Petersburg Creek.

The U.S. Forest Service rents 19 public cabins in the area. A couple are within hiking distance, but others require float planes or boats. Contact the Petersburg Ranger District.

A network of logging roads beginning at about Mile 11 loops to Three Lakes Recreation Area on the east side of the island and back to about Mile 21. Shelters, picnic sites, trails and views of Frederick Sound are available. Tracts of old and recent logging sites are visible along the road. Ask for a map from the Forest Service or visitor center.

Events

Little Norway Festival is a four-day whirl of costumes, dance, music, parades and food—lots and lots of Norwegian food. The event is held on the weekend closest to Norway's Independence Day of May 17. The wild bunch dress up as Vikings and Valkyries and roam through town stealing fair maidens and lads, meeting airplanes, engaging in water balloon fights with kids, and generally acting uncivilized. The more sedate don their elaborate folk costumes, some costing as much $2,000, for dances and fashion shows. People fill up with Norwegian delicacies and other dishes at a smorgasbord, pancake breakfasts, international foods dinner, salmon bake and Fish-O-Rama, and then they work off the calories with rowboat races, the Viking Ball and a street dance. The Mitkof Mummers present a melodrama each night with such titles as *Dirty Deeds at Dire Streets*, or: *One Fish in the Net is Worth Two in the Street*. Even if you're not Norwegian, you'll feel as if you were after the Little Norway Festival. Write to the festival committee at Box 649, Petersburg, 99833.

The Salmon Derby is held each Memorial Day Weekend, sponsored by the Petersburg Chamber of Commerce. Cash prizes sweeten the pot. Write the chamber for more information.

The Fourth of July celebration is an enthusiastic, small-town affair.

41

St. Michael's Cathedral dominates downtown Sitka.

Sitka

Ask around, and a surprising number of Southeast Alaskans would admit that if they had it to do all over again, they'd live in Sitka. Spend a moment looking over Sitka Sound, and you'll understand why.

In a state of uncommon beauty, Sitka is uncommonly beautiful. The triangular peaks of The Sisters frame the town, while a circlet of islands wreaths the cove. Mount Edgecumbe, a dormant volcano, interrupts the horizon with its Mount Fuji-like aspect. From its vantage on west Baranof Island, Sitka is the only community in Southeast that faces the Pacific Ocean dead-on. People often call it the more lyrical "Sitka-by-the-Sea."

Part of what gives Sitka its sparkle is the way it wears the heirlooms of Tlingit, Russian and American culture. The family jewels include the solemn totem poles of Sitka National Historical Park, the onion dome of St. Michael's Cathedral looming over downtown Sitka, and the Sitka Pioneers' Home. Under Russian rule, Sitka thrived as the "Paris of the Pacific," and the community still retains a certain cosmopolitan air by fostering major cultural events and renewed ties with Russia in ways profound and trivial. Where else can you buy a hamburger garnished with caviar?

But at heart, this is a small town, with about 8,500 residents. Only recently was a stoplight erected in town, and the first hapless motorist to receive a ticket for running the light received front-page coverage in the *Sitka Sentinel.* One of Alaska's all-time famous pranks took place here on April Fools Day in 1974, when resident Porky Bickar arranged for a helicopter to drop a load of tires near the bowl of Mount Edgecumbe where they were set afire. The black smoke gave folks the idea that the volcano was shaking itself awake, causing quite a commotion until residents real-

43

ized they'd been had.

As Jack Calvin wrote in his charming book, *Sitka*, you don't just move to Sitka—you enter into an apprenticeship as a Sitkan. After 20 years or so, you might be accepted as a full-fledged resident. Citizens new and old so cherish their community that the most divisive and longest-running battle in recent decades has been over the nearby Alaska Pulp Corp. mill. Spend enough time talking to a local, and the mill is sure to come up as a philosophical litmus test of jobs vs. environment. (The best course of action for visitors is to stay out of it.)

Given how attached people become to Sitka, you can understand why the Tlingits were none too pleased when the Russians sailed into Sitka Sound in 1799 to build a new headquarters for the Russian-American Company. The Kiksadi clan of the Tlingits had a fine appreciation of the area themselves, and in fact already lived at the best spot around in a village they called Shee Atika.

Chief Manager Alexander Baranov tried to do right by the Tlingits in the name of peace, so he built the original Russian settlement, New Archangel St. Michael, six miles to the north. From there the company continued harvesting "soft gold," the wealth of sea otter pelts and other furs that brought such a good price in China.

All seemed well until Baranov left town on company business for 18 months, during which the Tlingits torched the settlement and massacred everyone at hand. Only those hiding in the woods escaped to tell of the colony's fate. On his return, Baranov decided he would just as soon occupy the village site of Shee Atika he had desired in the first place. The clever Kiksadi, knowing the Russians would come after them, left their fort on Castle Hill and built another at the mouth of Indian River.

Sure enough, a Russian armada sailed into the sound with a fleet of 300 bidarkas, four ships and the gunboat *Neva*. When the wind failed, bidarkas towed the *Neva* into the cove. After failed negotiations, unsuccessful bombardment of the fort by the *Neva*, and a skirmish that came to be known as the Battle of Sitka, the Tlingits disappeared into the forest. The Russians torched the Indian village and re-established their occupation.

The town that sprang up in the wake of this conflict was like no other settlement on the Pacific Coast. Under the able leadership of Baranov, New Archangel became a major trading center along the Pacific Coast. Industries included shipbuilding, sawmills, flour mills, a tannery and a saltery. The Russians erected their own log fort on Castle Hill, and other institutions sprang up, including the Russian Bishop's House in 1842 and St. Michael's Cathedral in 1848 .

The governors who followed Baranov turned Sitka into a glittering colony for those with money and standing, but Sitka's glory was not to last. In spring 1867, Russia sold Alaska to the United States for $7.2 million dollars, or about two cents per acre, surely the greatest land deal in history. The transfer ceremony took place Oct. 18 on Castle Hill.

The new owners really had little interest in their property, and Alaska, along with Sitka, entered an era of benign neglect, as history books now term it. Until the makings of a civil government were established in 1884, Sitka barely hung on. Eventually the town stabilized and began developing with a sealing industry, salmon and halibut fisheries and later timber harvesting and processing. At the turn of the century, the territory's capital began a slow transfer from Sitka to Juneau.

Today, the Alaska Pulp Company mill at nearby Silver Bay is the town's major employer, but tourism and fishing fill in the gaps. Over the decades Sitka became the center of operations for a variety of organizations, including Sheldon Jackson College, the U.S. Coast Guard, and the Alaska State Troopers' training academy. Japonski Island served as a naval base for U.S. troops during World War II, and later the Mount Edgecumbe boarding school for Alaska Native high school students and a Native hospital were housed in converted buildings. The University of Alaska Southeast Sitka campus also is on the island.

Attractions

Sitka's history promenades throughout the town. A good introduction begins at the Centennial Building, near the cruise ship float at Crescent Harbor. The building houses the Isabel Miller Museum, named after a resident whose collections form the museum's core. A model of Sitka in 1867 depicts the town when it changed hands from the Russians to the Americans. Other displays include artifacts dating from the Russian occupation, Native arts, and exhibits on lumber and fishing industries. Look for the black bear fur muff in the Victorian exhibit.

45

Also in the Centennial Building is the Sitka Convention and Visitors Bureau, with plenty of maps, brochures and advice. The concert hall provides the stage for the New Archangel dancers, a renowned folk group who perform colorful traditional dances against a view of Sitka Sound. A collection of mounted animals occupies the other end of the building, including a rather tattered bear.

Castle Hill presents views of town, Sitka Sound and Japonski Island. Two entrances lead to Castle Hill State Historic Site. A spiral path suitable for handicapped access leads from a parking lot on Harbor Drive, near the bridge. A stairway leads from Lincoln Street, just beyond the pharmacy.

Baranov dwelled up here until 1817, first in a small cabin later replaced by a house filled with expensive furnishings, paintings, silver samovars, and an extensive library of fine books. His successors built a new residence by 1822 and later a two-story log mansion called Baranov's Castle. The enormous structure included the first lighthouse on the Pacific coast. The governors, as they were called, held gala balls among lavish furnishings and appointments, including a grand piano. The castle was said to be occupied by a ghost variously called the Lady in Black, the Lady in Blue, and the Lady in White. One witness said the specter wore a blood-stained wedding dress and cried.

Tears also were shed at the transfer ceremony held at the castle Oct. 18, 1867. To thunderous gun salutes, the Russian flag was lowered and the Stars and Stripes raised in the company of Russian and American troops, citizens, and Prince and Princess Maksoutoff, the castle's last Russian occupants. (Princess Maksoutoff never left Sitka; she is buried in the Russian cemetery.) In 1894, six months after American officials repaired the uninhabited castle, it burned in a spectacular fire. A later structure also burned. Today Castle Hill is the site of an annual re-enactment of the transfer ceremony each Alaska Day.

The imposing Sitka Pioneers' Home, at the corner of Lincoln Street and Katlian Street, was built in 1934 so long-time Alaskans could live in retirement or receive nursing care. Visitors can enjoy the lovely gardens and a gift shop selling crafts made by residents. The bronze statue on the lawn, "The Prospector," was modeled on William "Skagway Bill" Fonda, who embodied the frontier spirit of Alaska's sourdoughs.

In Totem Park, across from the home, stand reminders of Russia's enduring influence here. The totem pole is carved with the emblem of czarist Russia, the double-headed eagle. A more recent monument commemorates the 250th anniversary of the 1741 Bering-Chirikov expedition that discovered Alaska's existence. Inscribed in Russian and English, the monument was given to Sitka by a modern-day expedition of Russians who set sail for Alaska in tribute. Alaskans began renewing ties with their neighbors in the Russia Far East long before the Soviet Union disintegrated, and now citizens of both Alaska and Russia traipse back and forth regularly.

If you continue along Katlian Street, you'll pass the Pioneer Bar, a favorite hangout with fishermen and others. From the booths you can study wall-to-wall photographs of ships and fishing boats. Ask the bartender about the time the live rattlesnake appeared in the men's bathroom and was held off by bar patrons wielding pool cues.

Farther along the drive are old-fashioned Tlingit houses, some painted with clan designs, as well as a cold storage and cannery. The Mariners Wall above the Alaska Native Brotherhood Harbor on Katlian Street is a memorial to those lost at sea.

Returning to Lincoln Street, the town's shopping center, look for historical plaques explaining the significance of structures now housing stores. In the old days, Lincoln Street was known as the Governor's Walk and as the Russian Promenade.

Splitting Lincoln Street is St. Michael's Cathedral, a replica of the original cathedral built in 1844-48. When the doors swing open after a service, the incense of Russian Orthodoxy wafts into the brisk salt air; this is the church's seat in Alaska. Bishop Innocent, or Ivan Veniaminoff, designed the cathedral in the form of a cross facing east. Veniaminoff was something of a Renaissance man who arrived in Alaska in the 1820s as a young missionary before becoming bishop. In 1977 he was canonized as St. Innocent the Apostle to America. Bishop Innocent's great-great-grandson, a monk in Irkutsk, Russia, visited the cathedral in recent years. Except for his black beard, he was said to greatly resemble his holy ancestor.

Though still an active church, visitors are welcome during tour hours. The small donation is well worth the chance to admire what has been called the best collection of Russian icons in the Western Hemisphere. (An icon is an image of a biblical person or scene, meant to convey parables and messages to those who could not read.) The oldest icons, dating to the 17th century, are painted on wooden boards. They were later embellished with jewels and coverings of silver, gold, or copper known as riza. The precious metals do not outshine the transcendent beauty of the painted scenes.

Some of the artifacts were brought here from Fort Ross, Calif., in 1841, after the Russians sold out to John Sutter. Others were donated by local residents. A few on the front wall were retrieved from the frigate *Neva* after it sank in 1813 on Kruzof Island while carrying icons to the church.

Also displayed are elaborate wedding crowns worn by bride and groom, religious vestments, and bejeweled gospels, some weighing as much as five pounds. Ask the attendant to point out the mother-of-pearl cross that is said to harbor a sliver from the cross on which Christ was crucified.

The icons and other artifacts are all the more precious for having been saved by a chain of townspeople acting as a "bucket brigade" when the original cathedral burned Jan. 2, 1966, in a blaze that destroyed a good portion of downtown Sitka. "The saddest part was when the bells were ringing for the last time and went crashing down," says a church attendant. It took 10 years to rebuild the cathedral following the original blueprints.

Some parts of the church are off-limits to visitors, so ask before proceeding. Also, photographs and videos are not allowed.

A short detour up American Street, just before the cathedral, will take you to the Russian blockhouse and Russian cemetery. The replica block-house was built in 1960. Princess Maksoutoff's grave, worn by rain and time, is at the end of Princess Way. At the end of Observatory Street, directly above the cathedral, is the old Russian Cemetery, a wistful reminder that not all Russians returned to their homeland.

Continuing along Lincoln Street past Crescent Harbor, look for the yellow walls of the newly renovated Russian Bishop's House. For 16 years, National Park Service historians and architects labored to study and restore this structure, which served as home to 14 Russian bishops over 127 years, beginning with Bishop Innocent in 1841. The house is but one of four surviving buildings in the West that date to the Russian colonial era.

The bishop's house was a center of church authority that served as a seminary, classrooms and offices, and later as an orphanage, apartments and town library. Not until 1969 was it abandoned as a residence. By then age and rot had taken their toll. More than 70 percent of the structure is intact, however. Restoration revealed ingenious building techniques by Finnish shipwrights that helped the building survive. Also uncovered were more than 1,000 pieces of documents that had been cut into strips and glued to walls and ceilings to cover cracks in the wooden timbers. Before being re-covered, the fragments were photographed and are now being translated.

If you tour only the ground floor without waiting for the free guided tours of the upstairs, you'll have entirely missed the historical splendor of the living quarters, where most of the real treasures are displayed. Tours begin on the half-hour.

Visitors can peer into the bedrooms, pantry, dining room, and formal reception room, decorated with many original furnishings and restored to the building's 1853 appearance. Among the interesting items are a writing desk with secret compartments believed to be built by Bishop Innocent, as was the clock in the reception room. Other decorations and furnishings are authentic reproductions.

The Chapel of Annunciation is a place of simple beauty, where the plain wood walls and floor contrast with the rich fabrics and the radiant colors of the icons. All are original to the chapel, except the silver replica of the Last Supper above the Heavenly Gate. Though dismantled in the 1970s, the chapel was reconsecrated in 1988 and is occasionally used for services.

Near the Bishop's House and overlooking the harbor is the St. Peter's By-The-Sea Episcopal Church, constructed in 1899. The stone wall in the front of the church was built by Alaska's first Episcopal bishop, Peter Trimble Rowe, who traveled Interior Alaska by dog sled and snowshoe. His family plot is next to the church's front steps. Peer inside the church at the lovely wood floors, stained glass, and unusual lectern created by a carved eagle with outspread wings. A historical sketch in the alcove says the congregation tries not to have an "edifice complex" about the beautiful building, but it must be difficult not to be prideful.

The grassy strip fronting Crescent Harbor offers plenty of benches and covered picnic tables. You might need a rest before tackling Sheldon Jackson Museum, which is crammed with fascinating examples of Native culture within its octagonal walls. Jackson was a Presbyterian missionary

The Sitka National Historical Park features a pleasant walk through the forest with totem poles lining the path.

and educator who founded the Sitka Industrial and Training School, later to become the Sheldon Jackson School. In his travels throughout Alaska, Jackson gathered more than 3,000 items himself, including tools, clothing, masks, baskets and other artifacts representative of each of the major Native groups. He also gave money for buildings to house the collections, including the present concrete structure built in 1896. The State of Alaska purchased the museum from Sheldon Jackson College in 1985.

Highlights include the war helmet of Katlian, who resisted Baranov and company in the Battle of Sitka. A few tufts of bearskin remain on the wooden helmet. Kids are fascinated by the one-piece suit made of walrus intestine that was used for butchering whales but that looks more like a space suit. Don't forget to open the exhibit drawers to examine still more items. The museum is open daily during the summer. A museum shop sells postcards, books, and Native arts and crafts.

Sheldon Jackson College, founded in 1878 as a Native boarding school, is now a year-round educational center. Author James Michener lived at the campus for three years in a house on Jeff Davis Street at the invitation of the college while he was researching and writing the novel *Alaska.*.

A pleasant stroll beyond the college leads to Sitka National Historical Park, home to a tribe of totem poles scattered through the forest. Land for the park was set aside in 1890 by President Benjamin Harrison on the point where the Kiksadi fort was defended in the Battle of Sitka. From the original gathering of 18 poles, the collection grew as other totems, mostly Haida, were retrieved from outlying islands and villages. Many were replicated by Native artisans during the Depression-era Civilian Conservation Corps projects.

The park's visitor center includes an auditorium that screens a short presentation describing the Battle of Sitka. Among the display cases is the blacksmith's hammer wielded by Katlian. One wing houses the Southeast Alaska Indian Cultural Center, where Native artisans create totems and masks, silver jewelry and beadwork.

Along the Governor's Walk (also known locally as Lovers Lane), the poles stand bathed in the cool green light of the forest and the constant sound of the sea. The flat trail circles the point in a one-mile loop that parallels the beach. Along the way is the silent meadow where the Kiksadi fort stood in the 1804 Battle of Sitka. Park service staff lead guided walks.

An inexpensive booklet interpreting the poles may be purchased at the center and is recommended for those who truly want to appreciate the craft and character of the totems. Look for the Trader Legend Pole, a rare example of a ridicule pole carved to bring shame to someone who failed to satisfy a debt. The bearded man who tops the pole could very well be the offending trader.

A footbridge across the Indian River leads to another system of paths. Picnic tables, fire pits, and an exercise trail make this popular with local residents. At the point is memorial to Russian soldiers who died in the battle with the Tlingits.

Old Sitka is commemorated with historical plaques at about Mile 7.5 on Halibut Point Road. This was where New Archangel Saint Michael was established in 1799 by the Russians and then attacked three years later by the Tlingits.

Visitor Information

The Sitka Convention and Visitors Bureau maintains an office in Centennial Building on Harbor Drive. Write: P.O. Box 1226, Sitka, 99835. Call 747-5940.

The Sitka National Historical Park Visitors Center is open daily and offers brochures, presentations, a bookstore, and historical displays. Write: Superintendent, 106 Metlakatla St., Sitka, 99835. Call 747-6281.

The Forest Service office is at 204 Siginaka Way, Sitka, 99835. Call 747-6671. A kiosk near Crescent Harbor is usually staffed.

The *Sitka Sentinel* publishes a free visitor guide, *All About Sitka*, with articles and information on local services and sights. Write: 112 Barracks St., Sitka, 99835. Call 747-3219.

Contact Alaska Department of Fish and Game sport fish office at 304 Lake St., or call 747-5355.

Transportation

The ferry ride to Sitka is one of the most scenic, passing through straits so narrow and shallow that a low tide can delay the boats. The trip also offers a great likelihood of seeing wildlife ranging from feeding hump-

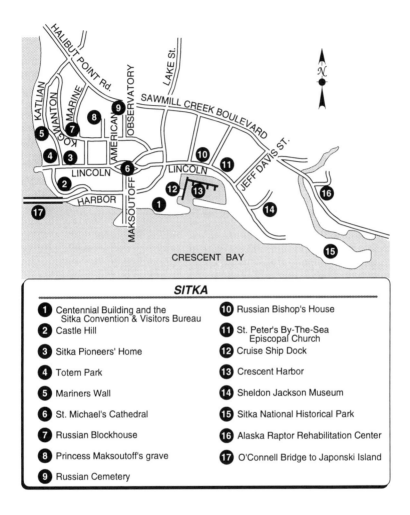

SITKA

1. Centennial Building and the Sitka Convention & Visitors Bureau
2. Castle Hill
3. Sitka Pioneers' Home
4. Totem Park
5. Mariners Wall
6. St. Michael's Cathedral
7. Russian Blockhouse
8. Princess Maksoutoff's grave
9. Russian Cemetery
10. Russian Bishop's House
11. St. Peter's By-The-Sea Episcopal Church
12. Cruise Ship Dock
13. Crescent Harbor
14. Sheldon Jackson Museum
15. Sitka National Historical Park
16. Alaska Raptor Rehabilitation Center
17. O'Connell Bridge to Japonski Island

backs to frolicking sea lions to floating sea otters, which only inhabit the outer coast.

The ferry terminal is located seven miles north of downtown Sitka. Bus and van services offer rides to town; they are usually less expensive than taxis. Call the terminal at 747-8737.

Major cruise lines wouldn't dare bypass Sitka, a favorite port of visitors. The lack of deep water close to town means cruise ships use lighters to transport passengers to the cruise ship dock.

The Sitka Municipal Airport is located a mile from downtown Sitka on Japonski Island, which is linked to town by O'Connell Bridge. Small air taxi companies and daily jet service is available. Juneau is 20 minutes away by air. The landing offers one of the most exciting in Southeast as it always seems that the plane is just about to smack into the water when the island runway appears. The airport is famous in the region for the lounge's daily roster of homemade pies. Don't be surprised to see flight attendants, pilots, or passengers boarding with a pie box in hand.

A couple of taxi companies in town compete for customers. Rental cars are available at the airport.

Sitka has four harbors, three with transient moorage: ANB Harbor, Thomsen Harbor, and Sealing Cove Harbor at Japonski Island. Check with the Sitka harbormaster on VHF Channel 16, or call 747-3439 or 747-3294.

Accommodations

Several hotels, motels, and inns offer rooms, ranging from budget to homey to luxurious. Bed-and-breakfast establishments are located throughout town. Ask at the Sitka Convention and Visitors Bureau in the Centennial Building for *Guide to Accommodations* for complete list of prices and addresses. Those craving the exotic can stay in a lighthouse on a nearby island. Boat transportation is included. Call 747-3056.

A youth hostel at 303 Kimshan St. is located in the basement of United Methodist Church. Check in at 6 p.m. and out at 8 a.m. No cooking. Call 747-8356 or write Box 2645, Sitka, 99835.

Four campgrounds are open to recreational vehicles, two of them catering to tent campers. For a complete list of RV and camping services in Sitka, ask the convention and visitors bureau for the brochure *Sitka: An RV Guide*.

Starrigavan Bay Campground with 30 sites is conveniently located about a half-mile north of the ferry terminal, at the end of Halibut Point Road. Nine camping spaces but no facilities are available free at Sawmill Creek Campground, about seven miles south of Sitka above the Alaska

Pulp Corp. mill. Turn left at mile 5.5 Sawmill Creek Boulevard, near the pulp mill, onto a gravel spur road and continue about a mile and a half. RV parking for 26 vehicles is available at the paved lot at Sealing Cove Harbor, located on the left just after crossing O'Connell Bridge to Japonski Island. The facility is run by the City of Sitka Harbormaster. The Sitka Sportsman's Association runs the Sportsman's Campground with eight RV spaces a block south of the ferry terminal. Call 747-8886 for reservations.

Excursions

Wake up early enough in the summer, and you'll see sport fishing boats zooming out to sea. Numerous charter outfits are more than happy to let you in on the fun.

Bird watchers won't want to miss expeditions to St. Lazaria Island, a 65-acre volcanic island populated by a half-million breeding seabirds. The wildlife refuge is located about 15 miles southwest of Sitka. Among the more unusual waterfowl are tufted puffins and rhinoceros auklets, which burrow into the ground. Foot traffic is discouraged because oceanic swells make landing difficult and nest sites crowd the island. Contact U.S. Fish and Wildlife Service at 747-8882.

Other charters take passengers looking for humpback whales, sea otters, sea lions, and other wildlife. Wildlife is so abundant here, in fact, that one tour company advertises that passengers who don't see an otter, whale, or bear will receive half their fare in refunds. Cruise tours of the coast around Sitka, including the pulp mill, are also offered. Check at the visitor center.

Entertainment

The New Archangel Dancers, composed entirely of women, have entertained visitors for more than 20 years with Russian and ethnic folk dances. Performances are staged regularly in Centennial Hall; check there for show times and ticket prices.

Shoppers will have no problem keeping busy among Sitka's galleries and gift shops. Many feature authentic Russian items, including icons, enameled boxes, china, pins, and nesting dolls.

Outdoors

With only 34 miles of paved roads, you can be sure Sitka residents have figured out ways to amuse themselves. Outdoor activities are high on the list.

The Forest Service Sitka Ranger District makes 19 cabins available for public use, many of them built by community volunteers. Some require float planes or boats for access. The Lake Eva cabin makes fishing and overnight stays easy for those who use wheelchairs. Check with the Forest Service.

Picnic areas here offer great views of Mount Edgecumbe or the island-studded waters. Pioneer Park is about two miles north of town on Halibut Point Road. Halibut Point Recreation Area, about five miles north of Sitka, includes a network of trails through the forest and good beachcombing (look for the beach where every rock is smooth and rounded). Both sites are state parks.

There are more miles of hiking trails than road here. A popular choice is Indian River Trail, a five-mile stretch that follows a stream through forest and bog to a waterfall. The trail begins at the end of a gravel road next to the Public Safety Academy on Sawmill Creek Road. The more ambitious can tackle Gavan Hill, Mount Verstovia Trail ("verstovia" means Russian mile) or Mount Edgecumbe trail. Shorter hikes lead to Thimble-berry Lake or Beaver Lake. Check with the Forest Service.

Events

The All-Alaska Logging Championships draw loggers from the Pacific Northwest each June for lumberjack contests, including chopping, speed-climbing, axe-throwing, tree-topping and choker-setting. Some events include women contestants, most notably the rolling pin toss. Check with the visitor's bureau.

The Sitka Summer Music Festival treats audiences to nearly a dozen concerts of chamber music in the span of three weeks. Founded by violinist Paul Rosenthal, the festival gathers some of the world's finest classical performers. The concert setting is unequaled, as performances take place before a glass wall that overlooks the cove. Write: P.O. Box 201988, Anchorage, 99520. Call 688-0880.

The Sitka Symposium invites writers, poets, storytellers and others for a week of readings, lectures and seminars on writing and humanities each June. Many of the faculty are critically or nationally renowned authors. Write: The Island Institute, Box 2420, Sitka 99835.

Alaska Day, Oct. 18, is a state holiday celebrating the territory's purchase by the United States, but Sitkans naturally feel somewhat proprietary about the whole affair, since this is where the transfer took place. The three-day event includes a parade, pageants, a costume ball, and a re-enactment. Contact the visitor bureau.

Sitka jumps into the fishing fray with its own five-day Salmon Derby, stretching over Memorial Day and the first weekend in June. Write: Salmon Derby, Box 1200, Sitka, 99835.

Sitka Raptor Center

S oaring and dipping over the calm green waters of Crescent Cove, nearly two dozen eagles take turns trying to snatch something from the water that seems promisingly like food. When one of the eagles finally retrieves the dead fish, the others flap back to their perches in the spruce trees lining the shore to await the appearance of another meal.

But up the hill, at the Alaska Raptor Rehabilitation Center, an immature eagle named Mars will never soar again. Discovered in spring 1992 with a serious compound fracture, her left wing had to be amputated.

Inside the center's clinic, visitors watch through a large window as volunteers carefully remove Mars' old bandage, painstakingly clean the stump and replace the covering. The hooded bird occasionally struggles and twitters.

"OK, girl. This will be all over in a little bit," soothes the woman firmly holding the eagle.

Mars was one of 33 injured eagles brought into the center by the end of June 1992—about twice the usual rate. "They just keep coming in," a staff member says. At the raptor center, at least there's hope for these proud birds. The center functions as a hospital for injured eagles and other birds of prey, such as hawks and owls. Most are found by fishermen, hikers, and other folks in Sitka and outlying areas.

About 80 percent of the eagles were injured in encounters with humans. Among the causes of injuries are gunshot wounds, ingested fishing hooks or lines, poison, traps and collisions with cars, telephone wires, and other structures. Some eagles simply have a tough time making it through the winter and are brought in weakened and underweight.

Despite valiant efforts, many rescued eagles die. About 40 percent of

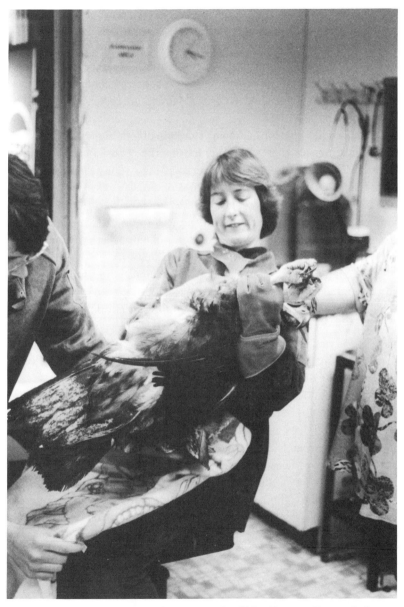

Wearing leather gloves, a volunteer at the Sitka Raptor Center helps secure a fiesty bald eagle which is about to receive medical treatment.

the patients recover and are released back to the wild, according to the center. Others, like Mars, can never leave. They'll live here or be transferred to zoos, veterinary teaching hospitals, universities, captive breeding programs, or other facilities where they can contribute to raptor knowledge or to eagle populations in the Lower 48. Sometimes people who see these survivors elsewhere send letters and photos to the raptor center to show how former patients are faring.

Some eagles become community teaching birds. Buddy, a male eagle recovered from Kake as a juvenile, has imprinted on humans and would never survive in the wild. His unnatural affinity with people makes him ideal for classroom visits and other projects.

The center outgrew its roots as a backyard project in 1980 to become a non-profit corporation and community project. In 1990, the program moved into its present building, which includes a clinic, offices, classroom and auditorium. Recovering birds stay in nearby mews.

The raptor center relies on help from volunteers to survive. In 1991, for example, volunteers donated nearly 4,500 hours to cleaning mews, feeding birds, exercising convalescents, doing paperwork, and other tasks. Local businesses and residents donated supplies, money, and fish. Veterinarians and physicians contribute expertise. As a private organization, the center does not receive any government funding and depends on the financial generosity of visitors, members and corporations.

"The reward is not in the form of money. It is something quite precious," a volunteer says. That payment arrives when volunteers, staff and community members gather to set a recovered bird free, sending it back to the forest and ocean where it belong.

The center includes a gift shop, video presentation, gallery of patients, and four owls kept as educational birds. Free open houses for visitors are held regularly throughout the week. Donations are requested, and visitors also are invited to join the center as members. More extensive guided tours of the clinic and eagle mews are offered a few times a week for an admission fee. The center also publishes a quarterly newsletter.

Call the center at 747-8662 for tour times, or write P.O. Box 2984, Sitka, 99835, for more information. The center is located off Sawmill Creek Road between the state trooper academy and the post office.

Juneau

It is the best of towns. It is the worst of towns. That's how Alaskans tend to divide in their opinions of Juneau, Alaska's capital city. Those who live here enjoy its combination of sophistication, small-town atmosphere, and wilderness. Juneau can be so appealing, in fact, that *Outside* magazine recently named it one of the 10 best communities in the country (causing residents to fear an influx of trend-mongers).

Juneau's detractors don't think of it as the country's prettiest capital city—they consider it the country's soggiest and most remote capital city. Their arguments were so persuasive, in fact, that Juneau spent much of the 1970s and '80s fighting to keep the capital right where it has been since the turn of the century. The battle to move the Legislature closer to Alaska's largest city, Anchorage, was so bitter that people still wince when the subject surfaces.

The good thing about Juneau is that it can accommodate just about anyone's philosophy. The 30,000 residents really occupy different Juneaus. Some live in the Juneau where people sip espresso, attend avant-garde productions of the prestigious Perseverance Theatre, and listen to jazz ensembles. Others live in the rarefied air of politically-charged Juneau. Still others fish in the summers, hunt in the fall, and wear rubber boots the year-round in the outdoor Juneau.

Juneau's undergone several personality changes ever since gold brought it to life in 1880, thanks to two raffish but veteran prospectors by the name of Joseph Juneau and Richard Tighe Harris. It was a member of the nearby Auke Tribe, Cowee, who led them by the nose up boisterous Gold Creek into the valley where he had seen gold.

61

Mt. Juneau overshadows downtown Juneau.

Their discovery of rich prospects in Silver Bow Basin alerted about 40 prospectors in the region, who immediately high-tailed it to Gold Creek to set up camp and record their claims before winter set in. The rough camp at the foot of Mount Juneau quickly grew into a real town as steamers and other vessels brought merchants, families, and more prospectors.

At first the town was called Harrisburgh, not too surprisingly, as Dick Harris named it so. Then the miners voted to name the camp Rockwell after the Naval commander who assumed civil authority in the first year. Postal officials were confused still further when the community was renamed Juneau, after old Joe convinced fellow prospectors (aided by with the liberal application of drink) that something really ought to be named after him.

The 160-mile Juneau Gold Belt fueled the town's economy for the next 65 years. Between 1881 and 1944, this stretch of gold-bearing ore produced 6.7 million ounces of gold and 3.1 million ounces of silver. The easy gold played out in a few years, and companies took over hard-rock mining. Three giant operations in Juneau grew out of these efforts, two of them becoming the largest gold mines in the world at that time.

The first was the famous Treadwell Mine complex on Douglas Island, with some shafts extending up to 2,400 feet out under the sea. For a time Treadwell was an incorporated company town that offered its 2,000 employees boarding houses, stores, a 15,000-volume library, a swimming pool, darkroom and gymnasium. Disaster struck in 1917 when shafts collapsed, flooding three of the four mines and swallowing several buildings. Miraculously, no workers died; the only man unaccounted for was believed to have taken advantage of the incident to disappear. In 1926, a major fire in Douglas swept away much of the complex, but relics still litter the beach and forest on Douglas. The Juneau Douglas City Museum sells an inexpensive walking tour map of the area's relics.

The Alaska Gastineau Mining Company operated just south of Juneau at a place now called Thane, after mine superintendent Bart Thane. Opening the mine required Herculean feats of engineering, including building the still-standing Salmon Creek Dam, the largest of its kind at the time, and digging a tunnel 10,500 feet through Mount Roberts, for years the longest tunnel in the Western Hemisphere. Despite innovative mill workings, technical problems and other troubles closed the company in 1921.

The Alaska-Juneau Mine, a couple of miles south of downtown Juneau, evolved in 1915 from companies that mined the Silver Bow Basin in the late 1890s. The mine soon dominated Juneau business, especially as the other mines closed. In 1944, a manpower shortage, fixed gold prices, and rising costs shut the A-J down. In 1965, a fire reduced the mill to the rusting hulk now visible on the flank of Mount Roberts. Some Juneau residents still remember working in the A-J.

After the war, the burgeoning territorial government grew to become the town's major source of employment. Fishing, lumber, tourism, and commerce all played important roles, but government work reigned. After voters rejected the capital move initiative in 1982 because of the expense, Juneau's economy boomed in sheer relief. Following a typical frontier cycle, the town's economy busted a few years later when oil prices fell and state workers were laid off. It has since stabilized, making Juneau a lively, thriving city.

The town has come full circle with a recent revival in mining. The Greens Creek Silver Mine opened about 18 miles west of Juneau on Admiralty Island and is presently the largest silver mine in North America. The miners commute to the operation daily on large catamarans that are berthed next to the state ferry terminal at Auke Bay. The mine company employs more than 250 people.

Several other mines in the region are being explored for development. A Canadian gold company subsidiary named Echo Bay Alaska hopes to reopen the A-J Mine and, with a partner, the Kensington Mine, which is about 45 miles north of Juneau. The proposals have caused a deep rift between residents for and against the mine. You will probably see bumper stickers proclaiming the drivers' sentiments: "Juneau is fine without the A-J mine" or "Import miners, export whiners."

It just goes to show Juneau is a town for all kinds of people. Downtown residents live in gracious renovated homes creeping up the hills like a miniature San Francisco. Most of the town's population lives in the Mendenhall Valley, nine miles northwest of town, which has been suburbanized with its own shopping centers, schools, and residential areas. Other folks live in enclaves at Lemon Creek, Auke Bay, Lena Loop, and Tee Harbor, or along the 40 miles of road extending north. Across Gastineau Channel on Douglas Island is the community of Douglas. Though officially embraced by Juneau's borough form of government, Douglas maintains its own prickly identity.

Attractions

Juneau's main attraction, of course, is the Mendenhall Glacier. (See sidebar.) Few people escape town without snapping a roll of film or three of this sight, since the road system makes this one of the most conveniently-located glaciers in the state.

Most visitors begin with a tour of downtown Juneau, a cluster of shops, restaurants and bars squeezed into a seven-block historic district. The district includes 143 buildings builtbefore 1914, with 60 of those dating before 1904. In an effort to widen Juneau's appeal to the growing number of tourists, the city has spruced up the streets, added a waterfront park, and generally primped itself up with flowers and banners. Many of the older buildings, which range in style from Queen Anne to Victorian to art deco, were renovated or restored by private owners.

On the Marine Park wharf, look for statues commemorating hard-rock miners, the USS *Juneau*, and Patsy Ann, a remarkable dog famous for meeting cruise ships in the 1930s and '40s. (See sidebar). The mural on the waterfront side of the Marine Park garage represents an amalgam of Juneau's past and present. Local artist Dan DeRoux based the painting on a 1887 photograph of thc steamer *Ancon* and its passengers, but he used modern descendants of 32 pioneer families as models. The Juneau Public Library located on top of the garage, presents great views of downtown Juneau, Douglas, and the Gastineau Channel.

South Franklin Street forms the liveliest part of Juneau's history. The buildings on the waterfront side of the street once hung over the tidelands on pilings. Many of the buildings along the street began life as saloons and dance halls, and you'll notice that some still house bars. Juneau's red light district thrived along this street from 1881 to 1954, making it Alaska's longest running, not to mention largest, such district. A former lady of the evening once said South Franklin was the real gold mine in Juneau. Longshoremen, fishermen and especially the miners lived and played in boarding houses, pool halls, steam baths, speakeasies and houses of ill repute. The sporting ladies worked in cribs, or small rooms, above cigar stores that offered a legitimate front. In the old gold rush days, the best-looking gals dressed up and sat in the front windows as advertisements. Some of these women later married and became respected citizens.

Most visitors stop for at least a photo of the Red Dog Saloon, conveniently located next to the Juneau Police Department and the wharf. Though not historic, the bar is popular with visitors because of its frontier atmosphere.

The Alaskan Hotel and Bar, 167 Franklin St., boasts a genuine historical lineage. Opened in 1913, it is the community's oldest operating hotel and is listed on the National Register of Historic Places. The period decor inside makes this a favorite spot for schmoozing by politicos.

Also on Franklin Street is the Emporium Mall, located in the Alaska Steam Laundry Building. Built in 1901, the structure's distinctive turret has marked downtown Juneau over the decades. It's worth wandering inside the mall to study the numerous enlarged photographs of Juneau's early days.

The flamboyantly purple Elks Building at 109 S. Franklin served as the first Territorial Legislature in 1913. Incidentally, the legislature's first bill gave women the right to vote seven years before the 14th Amendment was enacted.

The Imperial Bar and Cafe on Front Street may seem a little weary, but it comes by it honestly. A saloon has operated here since 1891, when the Missouri Saloon opened on this spot. The famous Louvre succeeded it five years later, making this the oldest bar site in Alaska, as near as anyone can tell.

The Valentine Building at 202 Front St. is a more elegant reminder of early Juneau. Built by Emery Valentine, who was a one-legged jeweler, six-time mayor, founder of the volunteer fire department and all-around character, it was finished in 1914 and is listed on the National Register of Historic Places. This lot was first staked by Pierre "French Pete" Erussard, who discovered the Treadwell gold holdings that vaulted Juneau to such prominence.

Directly facing the Valentine Building at 225 Front Street is a building that for nearly its entire life housed hardware businesses. When the *Princess Sophia* struck Vanderbilt Reef 30 miles north of Juneau in 1918 and sank with its 353 passengers, many of the bodies were brought to a makeshift morgue in the upper story of this building.

Davis Log Cabin at Third and Seward serves as the Juneau Visitor Information Center. The structure is a replica of the town's first church of

1881. Later incarnations included a school, carpentry shop, and brewery office. There's been talk of demolishing the cabin because of wood rot, and of building a center closer to the docks, so check at the Marine Park kiosk for information.

Fourth Street was the site of one of Juneau's most notorious murders in 1909. In a small cabin no longer standing, Robert F. Stroud killed a customer of his girlfriend, Kittie O'Brien. Stroud was known then as the "Peanut Kid," but in prison he earned another nickname—"The Birdman of Alcatraz."

The Alaska State Capitol was built in 1931 with pillars made from marble quarried from Prince of Wales Island. The governor works on the third floor, and the legislature meets here at the beginning of each year and then argues its way through May or thereabouts. Guided tours are offered in the summer; check inside with the security guard for times. Historic photos line the walls.

The Juneau Douglas City Museum on Fourth and Main streets is small but informative, concentrating on Juneau's gold mining history with a variety of artifacts, photographs and displays. Other exhibits highlight local Native culture, shipping industry and canneries. Free walking tour brochures highlighting Juneau's historic buildings and totem pole are available. The museum is open daily in the summer. A small donation is requested.

Those with the energy to walk uphill a block to 326 Fifth St. will find St. Nicholas Church, the oldest original Russian Orthodox church in Southeast Alaska. The octagonal church will celebrate its 100th anniversary in 1994. Many of the icons inside date to the 19th and 18th centuries.

After you catch your breath, continue still farther uphill to Seventh Street, known as Chicken Ridge in the old days. One reason was said to be the number of ptarmigan, or "chickens" in local parlance, that miners stalked for the dinner pot up here. Many of Juneau's grand old dames gaze out over the city from this ridge. Mine officials and town leaders lived in the Victorian mansions, while mine workers lived on neighboring Starr Hill or in small dwellings along the streets below.

The House of Wickersham, at 213 Seventh St., was the home of Judge James Wickersham in his later years. A man of many talents, he served the territory as a lawyer, judge, historian, writer, and delegate to Congress. The state operates the house as a museum preserving the judge's furniture, photos, diaries, and collections. Tours are available in the summer.

Back at the city museum, continue exploring by crossing to the stone edifice of the State Office Building. (Go ahead and call it the SOB; everybody else does.) Inside the lobby, which is at street level from this entrance, you'll find the state historical archives, state library, and the Old Witch Totem pole, the oldest in the city. The massive Kimball pipe organ once entertained theater-goers, but now it receives a musical workout each noon Friday when local organists play free concerts. The outdoor plaza on this floor offers a fine overlook of Gastineau Channel.

Continuing down Calhoun Avenue affords a view of the rest of Juneau. Snuggled against the bluff are remnants of Indian Village, where the Auke people settled after they moved to Juneau from their tribal houses 14 miles north of Juneau. The large building dominating the village is the Andrew Hope Alaska Native Brotherhood Hall. The Alaska Native Brotherhood and Sisterhood were instrumental in obtaining rights for Southeast's Native peoples long before it became an issue elsewhere in the state. (Hint: If you take the stairway from here down to Willoughby Avenue, walk past the ANB building, and then make a left onto Whittier Street, you'll find the Alaska State Museum.)

Farther down Calhoun Street is the Governor's Mansion. The colonial-style residence was completed in 1913 and dedicated with a community party. It is not open to the public, but Juneau residents line up every Christmas season for a handshake with the state's First Couple and free cookies at a traditional holiday open house.

Calhoun Avenue dips past some of Juneau's stateliest homes to cross Gold Creek. To the right is Cope Park, a pleasant spot to picnic, walk dogs, or admire the icy blue waters of the untamed creek as it tumbles from the high country into a concrete chute.

Keep walking on the left side, along Irwin and Martin streets, and you'll soon encounter shady Evergreen Cemetery. Joe Juneau and Dick Harris died elsewhere, but civic-minded residents brought them back for burial here. Cowee was traditionally cremated in 1892 but is memorialized at the cemetery. For an introduction to a handful of other Juneau characters, tour the graveyard with the *Evergreen Cemetery Historical Walk* brochure available from the visitor center.

Visitors shouldn't miss the Alaska State Museum at 395 Whittier St.

One of the state's finest repositories, it houses valuable collections representing Alaska's Native peoples, Russian era, and natural history. An unusual exhibit is a walkway that spirals upward around a simulated eagle nesting tree, allowing visitors a bird's eye view of the nest and residents. A major summer exhibition is planned each year especially for visitors. The museum is open daily in the summer.

Juneau is so spread out that many of its major attractions lie outside the downtown district. A popular tour bus stop is the Gastineau Hatchery, operated by Douglas Island Pink and Chum, Inc., at Mile 3 Egan Drive. Each summer the 450-foot-long outdoor fish ladder is wall-to-wall fins with returning king, coho, pink, and chum salmon. If you time your visit right, you may see a purse seiner harvesting returning salmon just off shore as sport anglers crowd the public dock. The lobby houses numerous salt-water aquariums bright with strange creatures from the depths, including starfish, sea cucumbers, clams, sea urchins, sea anemones and more. A huge vertical aquarium holds specimens of salmon, halibut, king crab, cod and other deep-sea denizens. Other exhibits include an enormous mounted bear, a bald eagle, and a simulated wheel house. A small marketplace sells a variety of fish products, including locally-produced salmon leather, canned salmon, and fish art.

Just down the road is the Alaskan Brewing Co., which opened in 1986 using an award-winning beer recipe from a turn-of-the-century Douglas brewery. Tours of the micro brewery, at 5429 Shaune Drive, are offered Tuesdays through Saturdays from 11 a.m. to 5 p.m. on the half-hour. Thursday is bottling day. Call 780-5866.

Auke Lake presents a picturesque view of Mendenhall Glacier rising above the placid lake. The University of Alaska Southeast campus and Chapel-By-the-Lake overlook the scene. No doubt professors and preachers alike have a particularly hard task competing with the scenery. Guides inside the lovely log chapel will tell you about its history.

The Shrine of St. Therese is sheltered on a tiny island of tranquillity at Mile 23 Glacier Highway. Built in the 1930s from stones gathered at the beach, it can be reached on foot over a rock causeway. Bishop Joseph Raphael Crimont, Alaska's first Catholic bishop, is buried in a crypt below the simple altar. A self-guiding tour brochure, postcards, and other items are sold inside the chapel, which is open daily to the public. The rocky shores are popular with anglers.

City-owned Eaglecrest Ski Area challenges local skiers with downhill slopes and cross-country routes, and wows everybody with its views of surrounding mountains and Lynn Canal. The resort's most famous skier, Juneau-born Hilary Lindh, won a silver medal in the women's downhill event in the 1992 Winter Olympics. In summer, the drive into the mountain valleys is beautiful. Cross to Douglas Island and drive 7 miles on North Douglas Highway to the ski area turn-off.

Visitor Information

The Davis Log Cabin at Third and Seward has brochures, reference books, videos, maps and other information. Ask for *Attractions and Services*, a list of hotels, restaurants, activities, charters, stores, and other facilities. Call 586-2284 or 586-2201. Write: 134 Third St.-JT, Juneau, 99801.

The Juneau Convention & Visitors Bureau can be contacted at 369 South Franklin, Suite 201-JT, Juneau, 99801. Call 586-1737.

Call 586-JUNO for a 24-hour hot line detailing events.

The U.S. Forest Service Information Center is housed in the Centennial Hall Convention Center at 101 Egan Drive. The center sells maps and books, takes cabin reservations, shows nearly 20 wildlife and scenic videos, and hosts Native craft demonstrations. The center is open daily from 8 a.m. to 5 p.m. in the summer. Call 586-8751. The Juneau Ranger District Office is at 8465 Old Dairy Rd., in Mendenhall Valley. Call 586-8800. The Mendenhall Glacier Visitor Center is staffed daily. Call 789-0097.

The Alaska Department of Fish and Game has hunting and fishing information. Offices are located just off Egan Drive near the Juneau-Douglas Bridge, and in Douglas, next to the U.S. Post Office. Call 465-4116 for a weekly sport fishing report, or 465-4270 for information.

The *Juneau Empire* publishes a free visitor guide distributed area-wide. Call 586-3740. Write: 3100 Channel Drive, Juneau, 99801. The newspaper building also houses a fine collection of Alaska artwork. Call for free tours.

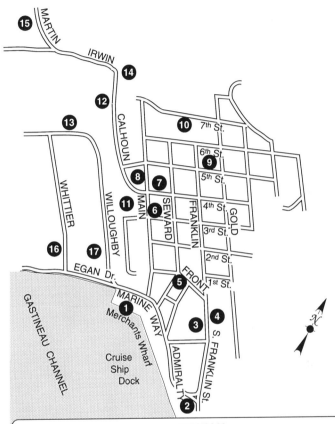

JUNEAU

1 Marine Park & Visitor Information Kiosk

2 Juneau Library

3 Alaska Steam Laundry Building

4 Alaskan Hotel & Bar

5 Valentine Building

6 Davis Log Cabin

7 Alaska State Capitol

8 Juneau–Douglas City Museum

9 St. Nicholas Church

10 House of Wickersham

11 State Office Building

12 Governor's Mansion

13 Alaska Native Brotherhood Hall

14 Cope Park

15 Evergreen Cemetary

16 Alaska State Museum

17 Centennial Hall & Forest Service Information Center

Transportation

The Juneau Airport was built on the only flat spot around, the Mendenhall Wetlands. Daily jet service to Seattle, Anchorage, Fairbanks, and points in between and beyond is available, as are the services of several small air carriers. On clear days, views of the Mendenhall Glacier are a bonus. Sometimes jet pilots will swing over the Ice Cap if conditions are favorable. Transportation by taxi, van, rental car, and public bus is available from the airport to downtown and other points.

The state ferry terminal at Auke Bay is 13 miles from downtown Juneau. Taxis and budget buses offer rides to town. The closest restaurants or accommodations are in the Mendenhall Valley, about four miles away. Convenience stores are located at Auke Bay, the terminus of the public bus system. During the day, if the ferry is docked long enough, buses will zip over to the Mendenhall Glacier to give continuing passengers a quick look. Ask the ship's purser if time will allow for such a trip.

The Alaska Marine Highway Office, where you can make reservations or buy tickets, is located at 1591 Glacier Ave., between Marie Drake Middle School and Augustus Brown swimming pool. Call the office at 465-3941 or call the terminal for schedule information at 789-7453.

Juneau is a major destination of most Inside Passage cruises. Ships berth along the waterfront or carry passengers to shore by lighter. Bus tours, both deluxe and budget, are available from the wharves, as are taxi tours and limousine service.

Juneau has four harbors, Harris and Aurora Basin near the bridge, Douglas Harbor, and Don Statter Harbor at Auke Bay. Transient moorage is available at Auke Bay and downtown. Call the harbormaster at 586-5255.

The Capital Transit public bus system has routes throughout the borough. Call 789-6901 or pick up schedules at the visitor center. Several rental car agencies operate, including in the airport terminal.

Accommodations

Motels and hotels are available near the airport and downtown. They range from chains to plush historic hotels and inns. Numerous bed-and-breakfasts establishments are located downtown and out the road, some on beaches. Ask at the visitor center for a list of establishments.

The Juneau International Hostel, open to all ages, is located in downtown Juneau at Sixth and Harris streets. Registration is from 5 p.m. to 10:30 p.m. Reservations are accepted by mail if accompanied by the first night's fee. Write: 614 Harris St., Juneau, 99801. Call 586-9559.

Juneau has little turning room and less parking downtown for recreational vehicles. Most shopping centers in Juneau allow overnight parking for RVs, and there are five parks that host campers. For complete information about services and to obtain municipal parking permits, stop by the Good Sam RV Info Center open daily in the Nugget Mall in Mendenhall Valley.

Auke Bay RV Park is private and is located 1.5 miles to the right of the ferry terminal and across from the Auke Bay post office. The year-around park has room for 25 vehicles. Call 789-9467. Norway Point Parking Area, with space for 10 RVs, is located next to Aurora Basin Boat Harbor downtown, about 12 miles from the ferry terminal. Turn into the harbor lot and then to the right about .2 miles. Savikko Park on Douglas Island has room for four RVs. Head downtown, cross the Douglas Bridge, drive two miles to Savikko Road and turn left into the first parking lot on the right. (Fees for the Norway Point and Savikko lots must be paid in advance at the Aurora Basin harbormaster's office).

The Mendenhall Lake Campground does not have electricity but does have room for 43 RVs, as well as tent campers. Turn right from the ferry terminal, drive 1.7 miles to the Loop Road, across from the Auke Bay harbor. Turn left and drive 3.2 miles to Montana Creek Road. Turn left and drive .8 miles to the Forest Service campground. Contact the Juneau Ranger District for more information.

The Auke Village Recreation Area offers 11 spaces for RVs, as well as tent camping. Turn left from the ferry terminal or drive 15.7 miles from downtown along Glacier Highway. Turn left at Point Louisa Road.

Dining in Juneau can be a real pleasure, whether you chomp on a bagel from a sidewalk vendor or sit down to a formal gourmet meal. Several establishments offer a wide range of surf or turf entrees and other fine dining. Cajun, Italian, Mexican and giant hamburgers round out the restaurant fare. To narrow down your choices, ask a local for advice.

Two salmon bakes offer all-you-can-eat fare and fresh fish. The outdoor Gold Creek Salmon Bake is located up Basin Creek Road in the historic surroundings of the mine district. Call 586-1424. The Thane Ore House offers an indoor menu at a beach-side building at Thane, four miles south of Juneau. Call 586-3442. Both operations offer free bus rides to their sites.

Excursions

Juneau is an ideal base for exploring the mountains, glaciers, islands, and marine environment that make Southeast so appealing. For information about specific destinations or tour operators, check with the visitor information center, or call the Southeast Alaska Tourism Council at 1-800-423-0568 or 586-5758.

In the ultra-spectacular category are flightseeing tours by helicopter or small plane cruises over the Juneau Ice Cap and through surrounding mountains. Helicopters land on glaciers so passengers can set foot on a river of ice. These tours are fairly expensive but offer stunning views.

Several cruises or flights to Glacier Bay National Park and Preserve are based in Juneau. Trips can be arranged through travel agents or at Marine Park tour booths.

Tracy Arm-Fjords Terror Wilderness Area is a little-known attraction easily reached from Juneau. The region resembles a miniature Glacier Bay, with dramatic gorges, wildlife galore, glaciers and waterfalls. Cruise ships, charter boats, and kayakers explore the fjords. Some tour operators offer fly-cruise packages to Tracy Arm, giving passengers a chance to fly over the Ice Cap one way and explore by boat the other direction. Others use small boats with shallow drafts to approach glaciers and wildlife with ease.

Raft tours down Mendenhall River offer mild thrills and the occasional chill. The 3.5-hour trips leave from Mendenhall Lake at the glacier, and after passing through a short section of rapids, float down the silty river, making a snack stop on a sandbar. (Hint: Go easy on whatever deadly concoction of liquors the guides serve as a warm-up.)

Several wilderness lodges are short flights or boat rides from Juneau. These establishments often include fishing or hunting guide services, as well as the chance to enjoy the wilderness in comfortable accommodations. Many people explore Admiralty Island from Juneau, as well.

74

Outdoors

Juneau spreads a rich smorgasbord of experiences for the outdoor enthusiast. Not even an entire summer is long enough to enjoy it all. Locals enjoy kayaking, hiking, camping, fishing, hunting, beachcombing, picnicking, sailing, and even golfing.

Kayak and bike rentals, as well as advice on local conditions and routes, are available from Juneau sport shops. Local kayak and bike organizations welcome visitors for club events. Ask at adventure or sport shops.

Many charter fishing operations offer half-day to week-long trips to local waters after king and coho salmon, halibut and other fish. Shore-bound anglers can take advantage of several fisheries managed just for them. Good spots include the public dock at Gastineau Hatchery, Fish Creek on Douglas Island and Sheep Creek at Thane, south of Juneau. Call the Alaska Department of Fish and Game sport fish office for tips and regulations. Fishing licenses are available at sporting goods and marine supply outlets.

The U.S. Forest Service manages four public cabins in the Juneau area that can be reached by hiking trails, some just a few miles long. Many others are located at lakes, islands and rivers in the region and require boat or airplane transportation. A directory, complete with photographs, descriptions and comments from past renters, can be examined at the Forest Service Information Center in Centennial Hall. Juneau cabins are named John Muir, Dan Moller, Eagle Glacier and Peterson Lake.

Juneau has one of the most extensive and well-maintained trail systems in the state. Trails ranging from easy to aerobic wind along Juneau's valleys, mountains and beaches. A valuable guide is Mary Lou King's *90 Short Walks Around Juneau*, which lists trails, beaches, and other recreation sites. *Juneau Trails*, published by the Juneau Ranger District, describes 26 trails in detail. Both publications are available at the Forest Service Information Center or in local bookstores. Pay attention to advice about weather and potential hazards (such as bears).

The municipality's parks and recreation department offers free guided hikes on Wednesdays and Saturdays, as well as transportation to the trailhead.

Call the department at 586-5226 for more information. Local businesses also offer guided hikes geared to client abilities. Lunch is usually part of the deal. Check with the visitor information center.

Several public beaches are ideal for picnics and beachcombing. Local favorites include: Sandy Beach on Douglas Island; the freshwater Twin Lakes, three miles north of downtown Juneau; and Auke Village Recreational Area at Mile 14 Glacier Highway, a beautiful crescent beach with numerous shelters secluded in the forest. Once the tribal site of the Auke people, the beach was said to be cleared of large rocks by slaves. Farther out the road are Lena Cove and Eagle Beach, both with outstanding views. All have rest rooms, shelters and fire grills. Numerous cameo beaches line the shore along the Glacier Highway. Look for pullouts.

Bird watchers will appreciate Mendenhall Wetlands Refuge, set aside because the estuaries and marshes are a haven for migrating and resident waterfowl. The refuge has several access points, including a roadside pull-out on Egan Drive. Ask for the brochure *Mendenhall Wetlands Refuge* at the visitor center for directions to other access points, or contact the Alaska Department of Fish and Game.

Photographers can't resist views of the Mendenhall Glacier from Brotherhood Bridge park, next to the Mendenhall River at about Mile 10 Glacier Highway. The meadow blooms with iris, Alaska cotton, and other wildflowers each spring. A trail leads from the meadow along the river to Montana Creek.

Amalga Harbor, reached by a left turn at Mile 24 Glacier Highway, practically oozes scenic vistas. Facilities include a public boat launch and rest rooms. The salt chuck is frequented by fishermen.

Point Bridget State Park is a remote treasure, which is the way its fans prefer it. Two different trailheads lead into the 2,850-acre park, passing through forest into an enormous grassy meadow that ends at a beach. Stunning views of Berners Bay, Lynn Canal, and the Chilkat Range make this park especially attractive. Ask for a park guide at the Alaska Division of Parks and Outdoor Recreation office at 400 Willoughby Avenue, or call 465-4563.

Echo Cove, at the very end of the road, is popular with campers and sun-seekers, though the only public facility is a boat launch. Some of the surrounding area is privately owned, so stick to the beach.

Golfers who want to say they've played within view of a glacier should try the Mendenhall Golf Course, near the airport on Industrial Boulevard. The course is challenging, with nine holes laid out across the wetlands. Golfers can rent rubber boots with cleats. Call 789-7323.

Entertainment

The Lady Lou Revue, performed by Perseverance Theatre, is a musical melodrama staged in Merchants Wharf, adjacent to Marine Park. Performances are offered in the afternoons according to cruise ship schedules, and in the evenings. Check the blackboard at the door for exact show times, or call 586-3686.

Janice Holst's *Golden Nugget Revue* performs nightly at the Thane Ore House. Call 586-3442.

Free concerts by local entertainers are scheduled every Friday evening in the shelter at Marine Park.

Several bars and saloons offer live musical entertainment. You'll quickly be able to tell from the clientele which are most suitable for visitors.

Events

Juneau hoots it up at the Fourth of July with a big parade and fireworks over the Gastineau Channel. The fireworks go off late in the evening of July 3, making them the nation's first. If you miss the parade in Juneau, rush over to Douglas, where it stages a reprise, followed by a firemen's hose race, Frisbee dog competition, street dance, and other events.

The Golden North Salmon Derby in August is sponsored by the Territorial Sportsmen to raise scholarship money for local students. The 100 largest fish earn prizes, with $12,000 going to the top angler. Ask the visitor center for details.

Each April folk musicians from around the state gather in Juneau for the Alaska Folk Festival, five days of public performances and workshops. Evening concerts give each musical act their 15 minutes of fame. Remarkably, it's all free. Write: P.O. Box 21748, Juneau, 99802.

Mendenhall Glacier fills the Mendenhall River with icy cold water.

Mendenhall Glacier

To visitors, the Mendenhall Glacier is a natural wonder. To Juneau residents, it's a playground. To scientists, it's a laboratory. For everybody, it's easy to reach—so easy that it's one of the state's top attractions.

Just 13 miles by road from downtown Juneau, the Mendenhall Glacier looms like a frozen ice sculpture over the Mendenhall Valley. Many residents jog, bike, roller-skate, or walk daily from their homes to visit the glacier's every-changing visage. The visitor center and outdoor shelter are favorite settings for wedding ceremonies and receptions. One couple even married on the glacier itself— giving new meaning to the phrase "cold feet."

The visitor center rests a half-mile or so from the face, separated from the ice by the silty Mendenhall Lake and mud flats. Telescopes allow a closer look, and a short, paved path leads to a photo point overlooking the face. Those who trek out along the lake's edge are cautioned that the ice is unstable, and large pieces can fall without any warning. (An ice fall crushed a woman to death not too many years ago.)

Trying to comprehend the Mendenhall's size and power is not easy. The face stretches 1.5 miles long as the glacier spills from between the mountains. The ice wall, which measures an average of 100 feet high, is a sort of time machine, revealing ice formed 150 years ago. The translucent, impossible blues are actually caused by the refraction of light from the incredibly compressed ice. Don't be disappointed if you visit on a cloudy day; the glacier actually colors more beautifully then.

A three-dimensional topographic model inside the visitor center puts the glacier into perspective. Indeed, it seems humble compared with the 1,500-square mile Juneau Icefield that feeds the 12-mile length of the

Mendenhall. The ice field is the fifth largest in North America, spanning gorges and valleys between impossibly sheer mountain peaks and spawning nearly 40 glaciers along the coastal range. For nearly 50 years, scientists and students have conducted studies for the Juneau Research Program at numerous camps on the glaciers.

Those who explore the area's trails will encounter markers pointing out the Mendenhall Glacier's position in previous decades. Until about 1750, the glacier was advancing. At its farthest point, the front edge extended about 2.5 miles farther down the valley, just past the present-day Loop Road. The retreat of ice has shaped much of the valley; for example, the Mendenhall Lake did not exist until after the turn of the century. Many residents remember how much closer the glacier was just 20 or 30 years ago.

The glacier area includes several points of interest. Spawning sockeye and coho salmon return to Steep Creek. Viewing spots are marked just before the parking lots. Bird watchers come here to see eagles resting in the cottonwoods, hear varied thrushes, and laugh at the American dipper, or water ouzel, an amusing bird that walks underwater to catch its food.

Several trails wind through the forested slopes to overlook the glacier. The East and West Glacier trails offer outstanding views of the ice and surrounding mountains. A moraine ecology trail loops across flat terrain, pointing out natural features left in the glacier's wake. A trail map and directions are available from the visitor center. Forest Service staff also lead walks on the moraine and to Steep Creek.

A small gift shop in the information center sells natural history publications, photographs and other items. Videos on the Mendenhall and other glaciers and wildlife are presented throughout the day. The center is open daily in the summer and is handicapped-accessible.

Major bus tours, taxis and small custom tours visit the glacier. The city's public bus line stops a mile from the visitor center. The walk, along a paved highway, can be a pleasant stroll as the glacier slowly reveals itself the closer you get. A helicopter or plane tour is an expensive but thrilling way to experience the Mendenhall and the mammoth ice field. Check with a travel agent or the Davis Log Cabin visitor center for more information.

Juneau's Patsy Ann

S ome towns erect statues of civic leaders. Juneau also remembers one of its most famous citizens with a bronze sculpture—Patsy Ann—the dog.

To look at Patsy Ann, you wouldn't think she was much of a dog. She had a skinny tail, pudgy figure, and blocky head. But in her time, some said she was the most famous canine west of the Mississippi, more photographed even than Rin Tin Tin. Patsy Ann had an unusual talent. Although deaf as the mountains, somehow this homely English bull terrier could sense steamers heading up the Gastineau Channel toward Juneau long before they blew their horns. Once she knew a ship was coming, she headed posthaste to the wharves to wait. It probably didn't hurt that passengers and cooks often gave her tasty scraps and the occasional steak.

Though a pedigreed dog with a perfectly good home, Patsy Ann seemed to think the whole town was her bailiwick. She spent nights at the longshoremen's hall, but she was not shy about inviting herself to social functions of all kinds. She kibitzed at card games, mingled at parish teas, and wandered into theater productions. Once she trotted out onto the field during a hard-fought baseball game between Juneau and Skagway teams and took charge of the ball. Everyone waited until she was done playing with it before resuming the game.

When the city cracked down on unlicensed dogs and sent Patsy Ann to the pokey, citizens chipped in and bought her a license. The longshoremen bought her a new collar. Eventually the town awarded her the title "Official Boat Greeter of Juneau."

The time came when Patsy Ann could no longer greet boats. On March 30, 1942, she died in her sleep at the age of 12. The next day, a large crowd paid its respects as her coffin was lowered into the Gastineau Channel from the Alaska Steam Wharf.

Patsy Ann has never been forgotten. An organization sponsored by the Gastineau Humane Society, "The Friends of Patsy Ann," solicited community contributions to commission her sculpture. Today, Patsy Ann greets cruise ships again from the Marine Park wharf. Her legacy is just as predicted by a writer named Carl Burrows in 1939: "Patsy Ann has not sought fame, but fame has come to her. Nor has she sought worldly goods, yet she never lacks for food or a place in which to sleep. But she has sought the friendship of all human beings, and far more important than fame, has gained the love and respect of the people of Juneau and occupies an enviable place in the hearts of all who know her."

Haines

Over the years, all kinds of people have fallen under the spell of Haines. The Tlingit Indians who settled the valley were the first, followed by Russians explorers, Presbyterian missionaries, gold seekers, fishermen, the Army, artists, nature photographers, and tourists. Hollywood even discovered Haines in 1990, capturing the area's gorgeous scenery on the big screen for the Walt Disney movie *White Fang,* and entertaining townspeople for months with their antics.

With this steady stream of pilgrims, it's surprising that many people consider Haines one of Southeast's best-kept secrets. Unfortunately, travelers often pass right through the small town in their anxiety to head north by way of the Haines Highway or south by way of the state ferry.

That's too bad, for Haines blends the best attributes of both north and south from its position at the joint between the panhandle and the pan. Endowed with the maritime and mountainous scenery of Southeast, it borrows the drier climate of the Interior. Thus, Haines enjoys less rain, more snow, and colder and warmer temperatures than its Southeast cousins (except for neighboring Skagway). This is one Panhandle town that has four bona fide seasons.

Accustomed to large numbers of folks just passing through, the 1,200 or so residents simply go about their business, often literally tending their own gardens, which grow very well here, thank you. They pride themselves on tolerance for the varied lifestyles led by a population that includes fishermen, artists, retirees, environmentalists, laborers, and members of a religious community.

The town of Haines feels no need to steal thunder from its setting on the cusp between Lynn Canal and the Chilkat Mountains. The streets are lined with rather plain buildings, many dating back to early days and now housing such modern innovations as video stores and pizza parlors. This is a place of rustic charms, where the local dentist hangs a wooden molar to mark his place of business, and a set of painted moose antlers hangs over the grocery store.

You'll find most of Haines' diverse attractions beyond these streets, where lakes, rivers, mountain trails, wildlife and seaside views lure outdoor enthusiasts. The most popular sight is the bald eagle, which can be spotted soaring up in the sky or perching in the cottonwoods along the Alaska Chilkat Bald Eagle Preserve. Though you will surely see some eagles in the summer, they gather by the hundreds and thousands in the fall and early winter along the Chilkat River. (See sidebar.)

Just like the eagles who gather along the river in tremendous numbers, the powerful Chilkat Tlingits grew strong on the valley's abundance and location. They gained power by controlling important trade routes through the mountain passes to the northern Athabascan Indians. The Tlingits exchanged oil from small fish known as hooligan, or eulachon, for furs and copper.

The Presbyterian missionaries gained a foothold in 1879 when the Chilkats awarded a chunk of land along Portage Cove to the church after feasting with missionary S. Hall Young and his traveling companion, naturalist John Muir. The early missionaries named their tiny outpost after a member of the church's mission board, Mrs. F.E. Haines. The bell standing outside the Haines United Presbyterian Church on First Street is the original sent to the new mission town in 1881.

In the 1890s, the rich Chilkat salmon runs drew some of the earliest canneries to operate in Southeast Alaska. Gold strikes at Porcupine Creek, 34 miles north of Haines, fueled a minor rush, although periodic flooding over the years caused problems. By then an enterprising fellow named Jack Dalton had convinced the Chilkats to let him use their trail over Chilkat Pass as a supply route to the Interior. When the Klondike gold rush started, Dalton charged a toll, asking 50 cents apiece for goats, sheep and swine, for example. Only Indians traveled for free. The Dalton Trail, as it was known, largely became the foundation of the Haines Highway. Dalton Cache still stands close to the U.S. Customs station at Mile 42.

Fort William Seward houses shops, restaurants and visitor services.

The temperament of sleepy Haines changed when squabbling over the border between the United States and Canada prompted the American government in 1903 to establish Fort William H. Seward at Haines on 100 acres of property donated by the Presbyterian church. Further changes came when the war-time construction of the Haines Cut-Off, now called the Haines Highway, linked the community with the Alaska Highway. The highway opened year-round in 1963, making Haines a popular transit point for travelers who want to combine a ferry trip with their road journey through the Yukon to Alaska. Southeast Alaska's maritime highway system began in Haines when one of Port Chilkoot's buyers, Steve Homer, used a World War II landing craft to transport vehicles, people and freight among Haines, Skagway, and Juneau. The territory bought his homegrown ferry in 1952 and later used the ferry *Chilkat* to seed its fleet.

A long-time resident once joked that Haines' major industry is worry. The economy wobbles with the fortunes of its main businesses. A sawmill recently closed, laying off more than a hundred people. Fishing is always an uncertain business, and visitors come when they feel like it, not when payroll have to be met. Many residents earn their living in ways as versatile as the early pioneers did.

In recent years, Haines has debated future development as a Canadian company attempts to open a world-class copper mine known as Windy-Craggy in northern British Columbia. The company hopes to use Haines as a port for transporting its ore to smelters, a strategy that would have tremendous effects on the tiny community. As agencies review the plans, residents are weighing the prospect of critical jobs against the specter of possible environmental and social problems that could harm their lifestyles or their fishing grounds.

Once considered the most powerful of Tlingit tribes, the Chilkats today continue their prominence as members of one of the state's wealthiest village corporations, Klukwan, Inc. Most members of the Native community live in Klukwan, a small village about 22 miles north of Haines. As their ancestors did, they gather hooligan in the spring and salmon in the fall. The residents prize their privacy and ask visitors to respect it by simply bypassing their town.

Attractions

A stroll around Haines will take you past the main visitor attractions.

A good start is at The Sheldon Museum and Cultural Center on Main Street. The exhibits are based on the collections of Steve Sheldon, a man of many talents and interests. Fortunately for him, his wife, Elisabeth, enjoyed collecting Native baskets, blankets and beadwork. The family treasures were shown at home and elsewhere around town before finding a permanent home in the museum in 1979. The building was a true community effort, built on land donated by the Presbyterian Church and funded with bake sales, hike-a-thons, grants and volunteer labor. One of the Sheldons' four children, daughter Elisabeth Hakkinen, directs the museum and lives in an apartment on the first level.

Sheldon's collections invest the museum with its personality. In a section called "Steve Sheldon's Attic," you'll see how wide-ranging his interests were. Items include everything from an armadillo skin basket to an ozone generator. Stuffed animals, photographic displays, and other artifacts fill the building's first floor. Look for Jack Dalton's sawed-off shotgun that he loaded with rock salt to break up fights in his saloon.

A reconstructed office displays many items belonging to town leader Solomon Ripinsky, a Polish immigrant who came to Haines in 1886 as a schoolteacher and worked in various enterprises. He also claimed 600 acres of land that later became the center of a long and tangled lawsuit with the city that left him poor. Notice the gravestone of his younger brother, Morris, which arrived with the name misspelled as Maurice. The display notes that Morris' wife didn't mind that so much, but the engraved cross instead of a Star of David proved to be too much for her to accept, and a second stone was ordered.

Upstairs the museum includes a small but insightful exhibit of local Native culture. Most notable are the Chilkat blankets, painstakingly woven in a characteristic geometric style by using dyed mountain goat wool entwined with strips of cedar bark. Don't miss the blankets created by Jennie Thlunaut, a master weaver who saved the technique from extinction by passing on her secrets to a dozen Native women before she died at age 96. The blankets are so prized that one student sold an intricate whale-and-eagle design for $20,000.

Other unusual artifacts include a set of nesting Russian trade goods trunks, made in China of camphor wood boxes and covered with rawhide, vellum and colorful designs. A rather diminutive, rusty cannon is one of four salvaged near the airport long after a Russian ship ran aground in the Chilkat River and was abandoned.

Other exhibits explain why the Chilkat Valley is such a haven for bald eagles. A 25-minute video, *Last Stronghold of the Eagles* is shown throughout the day, as is a show on Haines history. The museum is open in the afternoons daily during the summer, with hours extended for tours. Numerous information sheets on local history and culture are free. There is a small admission fee.

Those with an interest in frontier architecture will find detailed descriptions of local structures in a walking tour map available from the visitor center, or in a historical building survey sold at the museum. At the foot of Main Street, duck into the Harbor Bar and Lighthouse Restaurant to see a large, elaborate bar that once entertained gold seekers in Skagway.

As with other towns, the harbor at Portage Cove provides its own entertainment. Weekly commercial gill net openings mean you'll probably see somebody mending nets on the docks. You can often buy fresh seafood directly from fishermen here. Check the harbor bulletin board for announcements.

Stairways from Harbor Road lead into a grove of spruce trees where a small graveyard overlooks the cove. Faded stones date as early as 1898. Behind the cemetery is Tlingit Park, with play equipment, picnic tables, a bandstand, rest rooms and grills.

Lookout Park invites contemplation of the harbor and Portage Cove from benches and a covered kiosk. The monstrous contraption of gears and wheels displayed here is a steam mining drill used in Chilkat Valley at the turn of the century. An ideal stretch of sand for beach walking or picnicking begins at the kiosk and ends at the Port Chilkoot Dock. Stroll along the dock's boardwalk for panoramic views of Fort Seward and the town.

The orderly white buildings of Fort William Seward are most often photographed against the rugged white peaks of the Chilkat Mountains. The compound remains much as it did when troops drilled on the parade grounds, beginning in 1905. In World Wars I and II, the barracks served as training grounds for new recruits and later as a rest camp for seasoned soldiers. The fort was considered a foreign-duty post, with 400 enlisted men and 15 officers garrisoned at its peak. In 1922 the outpost was renamed Chilkoot Barracks to avoid mix-ups with the community of Seward. The garrison soldiers did not have much to do, really, and so enjoyed social and recreational pursuits in Haines. Some married local women and returned to Haines to live.

The fort had several notable residents, including a pet bear who learned to appreciate beer, thanks to the soldiers. Called "Three Per" for three percent beer, the bruin settled for ice cream cones when she couldn't bum a drink. Also well known was a captain's dog, Gus, who was said to eat steak every night. As for human achievement, Elinor Dusenbury, the wife of one of the colonels, wrote the music for Alaska's Flag Song as she was leaving Alaska.

After the Army decommissioned Chilkoot Barracks, five war veterans from the East Coast bought the compound's 85 buildings in 1947 with the idea of creating a new community. Their plans for Port Chilkoot, as it was renamed, did not succeed exactly as hoped, but along the way the families became part of Haines and the buildings began housing private businesses.

In 1970 the town voted to embrace Port Chilkoot as part of the City of Haines. Two years later the former post returned to its origins as Fort William H. Seward, a national historic site.

A walking tour brochure is available at the visitor center to identify the buildings' original purposes. The stately and well-appointed homes of Officers Row, most of them duplexes, are now private homes, bed-and-breakfast establishments or small shops. The smaller houses on Soap Suds Alley are bright with flowers and vegetable gardens. The street was so named because this is where wives of non-commissioned officers did laundry for the officers' families. Other structures house artists' shops and galleries, the Hotel Halsingland, Fort Seward Lodge, dog sled demonstrations and various enterprises, including a replica tribal house and trapper's cabin.

Not to be missed is the Alaska Indian Arts building, which still resembles the hospital it once was. Visitors are welcome to kibbutz as carvers, jewelers and other artisans work. Totem poles produced here have been sent to several world's fairs and are displayed in other states and overseas. Gift shops inside the building offer masks, jewelry and other items for sale. The nonprofit organization was founded by one of Port Chilkoot's original buyers, the late Carl Heinmiller, sparking a revival of Native arts in the area.

Haines bears a reputation as an artist's colony, with at least 40 local artists drawing inspiration from the Native culture and the wild setting. Look for their work in several galleries scattered throughout town. Haines also hosts a state and regional community theater festival every two years. The Lynn Canal Community Players, an amateur group active since 1957, produces the melodrama *Lust for Dust* as summer entertainment.

Visitors who won't be in Haines for August's Southeast Alaska State Fair may enjoy visiting the fairgrounds on the town's outskirts to see the reconstructed gold rush town, "Dalton City," which served as sets for the film *White Fang.* The making of the movie in 1990 turned the town topsy-turvy when a film company spent several months in Haines. Many residents donned period clothing as miners, trappers, dance hall girls and merchants to play extras or small parts. Others worked as carpenters, assistants and drivers. Much to the town's amusement, an unseasonable lack of snow in February forced the movie makers to create fake drifts by using mashed potato flakes and artificial snowmakers. Ironically, when the film was released in 1991, Haines residents were forced to travel to Juneau to see it because Haines has no movie theater of its own.

Information Services

The Visitor Information Center on Second Avenue, near Willard Street, is open daily with brochures, maps, and advice. Look for the row of flags. Ask for the *Haines Dining, Lodging and Recreation Guide* for advertisements of local businesses. A message board for travelers is available. Call 766-2234 or 1-800-458-3579. Write to the Haines Visitors Bureau at P.O. Box 518, Haines, 99827-0518.

The *Haines Sentinel Visitor's Guide* includes a walking tour, list of services, maps and other information. It is distributed free on ferries and throughout town, or write: *Chilkat Valley News*, P.O. Box 630, Haines, 99827.

The Sheldon Museum and Cultural Center on Main Street hands out free brochures and makes available campground and road guides for reference. The center is open daily in the afternoons. Call 766-2366.

U.S. Customs information is available at 767-5511. Canadian Customs at 42 Mile Haines Highway is open only from 7 a.m. to 11 p.m. Haines time. Call 767-5540.

The Alaska Division of State Parks number is 766-2292.

Transportation

The state ferry terminal on Lutak Road is about four miles from downtown Haines. Buses and taxis meet arrivals. Call the terminal at 766-2113 for schedules.

No jets land here, but small air services offer scheduled and charter flights to other Southeast communities. The Haines Airport is 3.5 miles from downtown. Ask for a ride from the flight company or call your motel.

Bus companies make regular trips to Anchorage, Fairbanks, Whitehorse, Denali National Park, and Skagway. A water taxi shuttles twice daily to Skagway, a good alternative to the ferry for people who want to zip to Haines' closest neighbor for the day.

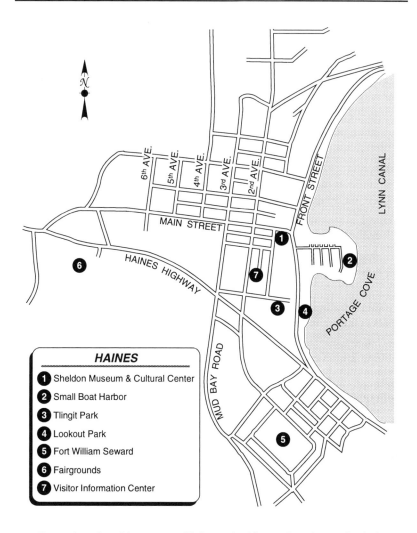

HAINES

1 Sheldon Museum & Cultural Center
2 Small Boat Harbor
3 Tlingit Park
4 Lookout Park
5 Fort William Seward
6 Fairgrounds
7 Visitor Information Center

Several cruise ships stop at Haines, docking at Lutak terminal, downtown at Port Chilkoot Dock, or anchoring in the bay. Company tour buses handle passengers.

Car rentals are available from a couple of motels.

The Haines Small Boat Harbor at Portage Cove and the Letnikof Cove dock on Chilkat Inlet have transient moorage. Check with the harbormaster at the small boat harbor or call 766-2448.

Accommodations

Nearly a dozen motels, lodges, and bed-and-breakfast places offer rooms for travelers. Five recreational vehicle parks are located on the shore of Portage Cove, near Fort Seward, on the outskirts of town, and at Mosquito Lake, 27 miles north of Haines. All have hookups. Some campers park at waysides along Lutak Inlet.

Public campgrounds are located in four state parks and recreation sites near Haines, although only bicyclists and backpackers are permitted to camp at Portage Cove State Recreation Site on Beach Road. Chilkat State Park, at the end of Mud Bay Road, has 32 spaces for tents and RVs. Chilkoot Lake State Recreation Site, at the end of Lutak Road, has another 32 sites. Mosquito Lake State Recreation Site offers 10 sites and facilities at 27 Mile Haines Highway. All have nightly camping fees.

Restaurants in town include a pizza parlor, Chinese food, seafood, and a bakery. A salmon bake operates in the replica tribal house at Fort Seward's Totem Village. All other visitor services are represented, including auto parts, gasoline, groceries, souvenirs, and even locally-grown organic produce, are sold in town.

Check with the visitor information center for specific information.

Excursions

Haines' climate and terrain is just different enough from most of Southeast to offer a dash of novelty. Many operators offer both saltwater and freshwater sport fishing charters—salmon and halibut in Lynn Canal, and Dolly Varden and salmon in nearby Chilkoot and Chilkat lakes. Such charters usually include opportunities to see marine mammals, eagles, bears and other critters. Buy fishing licenses at outdoor and general stores.

Natural history tours explore Chilkat Valley on foot and in vehicles, particularly seeking eagles. Jet boats and rafts wend their way through the Alaska Chilkat Bald Eagle Preserve along the braided strands of the Chilkat River. Adventure tours explore other rivers, glaciers, valleys and mountains in Glacier Bay National Park and Canada's Kluane National Park.

Tours also take in the Porcupine Mining District, an abandoned gold rush town. Specialized guides cater to photographers, hunters, and mountain bikers. Bike and kayak rentals are available.

Golfers may enjoy testing their skills on the challenging Weeping Trout Golf Course, 19 miles northwest of Haines. Privately owned, the course offers nine holes and eight artificial greens, with the fairways cut with chain saw and ax from the forest. The Weeping Trout Invitational Golf Tournament is held the second weekend in August. Lodging is provided at the course. Call 766-2827 for more information.

Flightseeing trips to nearby Glacier Bay and over the Juneau Ice Cap can be arranged through local air taxis.

For more information, check with the visitor information center or book trips through local travel agents.

Outdoor Recreation

Several trails explore both the shorelines and skylines of Haines. Challenging routes tackle Mt. Riley (elev. 1,760) and Mt. Ripinsky (3,920). Others wander along the beaches. A brochure, *Haines is for Hikers*, offers details and maps. Ask at the visitor center.

Even if you don't plan to camp overnight, Chilkat State Park is worth a visit for the views of the Chilkat Range and of two glacial neighbors, the hanging Rainbow Glacier and the Davidson Glacier. Take the Mud Bay road alongside Chilkat Inlet, past the small wedge of Pyramid Island and the historic Letnikof Cannery. From there the park road turns to gravel, with dips and curves extreme enough to warrant caution by RV drivers.

Outhouses, water, picnic sites and a boat launch are available, as well as campsites. A log information center includes natural history reference books and an ideal photo point of the two glaciers. The park is so quiet you can hear the waterfall thundering down the cliff below the Rainbow Glacier. A six mile trail ends at Seduction Point on the peninsula tip.

Ten miles from town at the end of Lutak Road, the Chilkoot Lake State Recreation Site attracts not only campers but boaters (there's a boat launch) and anglers, who wade into the shallow river after spawning salmon. Not to be confused with the Chilkat River, the Chilkoot River runs out of Chilkoot Lake, at the head of Lutak Inlet. Near the river's mouth is the historical site of Chilkoot village, which once had close to 500 residents. The Chilkoot Cultural Camp here each summer passes on traditions from elders to the young. On the road to the lake, look for Deer Rock, a Hondasized boulder on the river's shore commemorating peace negotiations between warring Tlingit clans. Deer were considered the most peaceful animal in the forest, hence the namesake rock.

A fish weir is located part of the way upriver so state biologists can count returning sockeye and coho salmon or tag them for studies. One day in late July, for example, the tally was 46 sockeye salmon for the day and 28,704 for the season. Anglers dot the shallow waters trying to catch at least one of those fish.

Entertainment

The Chilkat Dancers perform traditional Northwest Coast dances in costume three nights a week at the Chilkat Center for the Arts, located at Fort Seward. Call 766-2160 for show times.

Performances of the vaudeville show *Lust for Dust* are staged on weekends. Check with the visitor center for show times.

Events

The Fourth of July in Haines offers much of the same hometown enthusiasm you'll find elsewhere in Southeast.

In mid-August, the Southeast Alaska State Fair features five days of agricultural displays, competitions, horse shows, pig races, logging contests, and other events. People come from other communities in Southeast and the Yukon for the fun. The Alaska Bald Eagle Music Festival occurs at the same time, hosting concerts and dances played by nationally known musicians. Contact the visitor center for dates and information.

In January, events include the Alcan 200 snowmobile road race from the Canadian border to Dezadeash, and the Dalton Trail 30 sled dog race in the Chilkat Valley.

Alaska Chilkat Bald Eagle Preserve

B ald eagles are common in Southeast Alaska, but nowhere do they gather in such concentrations as at the Alaska Chilkat Bald Eagle Preserve, which borders the Haines Highway just north of town. In fall and early winter, as many as 3,500 eagles congregate along a five-mile stretch of Chilkat River where an upwelling of groundwater keeps the river ice-free and supports a large, late run of spawning chum salmon. From September through early January, this food supply attracts foraging eagles, who in turn attract large numbers of photographers.

The best viewing from the highway is generally between Mile 18 and Mile 22, along a stretch called the Council Grounds. It takes a moment for visitors to understand that the liberal sprinkling of white dots and dark shapes in the surrounding cottonwoods and along the sandbars belong to such an overwhelming number of eagles.

By January, the population of eagles dwindles to somewhere between 300 and 900 eagles. The eulachon run in late spring bumps the numbers up to about 500, but throughout summer just 200 or so eagles stick around. This means it is the hardiest travelers, willing to brave an Alaskan winter, who enjoy the glorious sight of hundreds of eagles roosting and feeding in a valley guarded by snowy peaks.

Alaska's population of eagles was threatened between 1917 and 1954 by the practice of paying bounties for dead eagles, which were thought to harm salmon populations. In four decades, bounty-hunters killed more than 128,000 eagles in Alaska. By the 1970s, researchers say, half as many eagles lived in Southeast as did in 1941.

In 1972 the state established the Chilkat River Critical Habitat Area to protect the main Chilkat population, but large areas of important habitat were not shielded when the state later contracted with a Haines logging company for long-term clearcutting. The valley became a battleground between local and national conservationists and those who supported logging development in Haines. The bitter strife divided Haines residents, but eventually a compromise led to the 1982 creation of the 49,000-acre Alaska Chilkat Bald Eagle Preserve to protect the most crucial habitat. Today, the preserve is a major draw for visitors each fall.

No visitor facilities exist in the preserve, but pullouts on the highway allow vehicles to stop safely. Local businesses offer tours and transportation to the preserve. Proper winter dress is a must, since rain, snow or cold temperatures can prevail. Remember that in winter, the best light occurs between 10 a.m. and 2 p.m., so plan accordingly. Contact Alaska State Parks at 766-2292 for more information about the preserve, or to apply for a permit if you want to do anything besides stand along the highway and take pictures.

Extensive information about eagles is displayed at the Sheldon Museum and Cultural Center, or write to the Division of Parks and Outdoor Recreation, 400 Willoughby Ave., Juneau, 99801. The American Bald Eagle Foundation is constructing the Dave Olerud Center near Second Avenue in Haines to promote research and tourism. For a checklist, *Birds of the Chilkat Valley*, ask at the Haines visitor center.

Skagway

There's more history per square foot in Skagway than in just about any other town around. Skagway still echoes with the crazy, glorious days of the Klondike Gold Rush because many of its most important buildings have been salvaged from the cruelties of time. Today, hordes of tourists washing up and down Skagway's streets give the town an air of discovery and excitement it must have worn just before the turn of the century. For Skagway, the gold rush was like a burst of fireworks, brilliant but all too brief.

A glimmer of all of that light still shines, though. Here you can belly up to the bar in a former brothel, ride a historic train along a trail of tears, or take a gander at Jeff Smith's Parlor, a forlorn little building that betrays nothing of the con man's legendary rise to power in Skagway or his death in a shoot-out. Jefferson "Soapy" Smith has come to represent the lawless and tumultuous history of the gold-rush era, but the truth is that Skagway was a town filled with interesting characters, for who but the most adventurous, most desperate, or most hopeful, would leave their lives behind in a wild chase for fortune?

Many of Skagway's 700 residents are descended from those who came seeking riches and settled for making a living instead. On a four-cruise ship day, times must not seem so different from 1898, when 10,000 people and more swelled town at the head of the Taiya Inlet. These days citizens rely on more than 300,000 visitors a season to sustain the community. In fact, they just about turn the town over to visitors, happy to see tourists arrive each spring and probably just as happy to see them go come fall so they can have their town back.

97

Wander beyond the bustle of Broadway Street into the neat residential blocks, and you'll have some inkling of the town's real life, where people putter in their gardens, play softball, and enjoy the long summer days. Skagway is known throughout Alaska and the Yukon for its rollicking Fourth of July celebration, but residents need little excuse for a social gathering. Officially proclaimed the "Garden City of Alaska," Skagway hosts an annual flower show and garden club competition to showcase the colorful yards, gardens, and flower boxes that perfume the air. Running races, snow machine races, and softball tournaments draw Canadians of a like spirit into town; in fact, Skagway holds a party on Victoria Day weekend in May just for their Yukon neighbors.

In winter, much of the town hibernates as many hotels and shops close for the season, giving townspeople plenty of time to conjure up a rousing good fight or two over civic matters—battles usually forgotten come spring. The town is quirky enough that Skagway's police blotter serves as entertainment for an East Coast radio station. (Sample entry: "June 30—A kid broke off a sprinkler head at the park and created another gusher.") Far from its lawless origins, Skagway finds major crime such an anomaly now that a minor rash of car thefts once prompted a resident to half-jokingly form a support group for other victims.

Despite its peaceful air, Skagway will never be as quiet as it was when Capt. William Moore decided to explore a secret pass through the forbidding mountains standing sentinel at the head of Taiya Inlet. With a Native guide, the 65-year-old adventurer hacked his way over the rugged route and decided it was promising enough to warrant claiming a 160-acre homestead in the valley. Some day, he figured, gold discoveries in the Yukon would require such a pass, and he would be ready to capitalize on his foresight by selling property.

No Tlingits lived there at the time, but they called the place "Shagagwei," a name variously translated but most commonly said to mean "windy city." As Moore's son, Bernard, wrote, "Skagway is a name very typical of a place where the same air is never breathed twice."

The valley was lonely no more when word of the fabulous gold strikes in the Klondike reached the world a decade later. Imagine Moore's chagrin when crazed gold seekers simply flooded the valley in waves starting on

July 26, 1897, paying no more attention to his ownership than they would to a gnat.

A crude tent city sprouting in August 1897 gave way quickly to a real town forming by December as thousands poured into Skagway, preparing for an arduous 600-mile journey over the pass and down the Yukon River to Dawson.

Skagway became one of two staging grounds into the Yukon. Neighboring Dyea settled at the foot of Chilkoot Pass, shorter but steeper than White Pass. It is difficult to imagine the struggle and torment experienced by the stampeders and their pack animals as they attempted to traverse these primitive routes into Canada, but the tales have filled many books, and the relics are scattered yet along the trails.

Those not trying to make their fortune in the Klondike were trying to make their fortune from the Klondikers. In addition to legitimate businesses, gambling, prostitution and saloons flourished at Dyea and especially Skagway. Innocents were fleeced of supplies and money; others were shot down in the streets. One authority simply called Skagway "hell on earth."

The ringleader of much skullduggery was Soapy Smith, a gambler, con artist and all-around bad guy who virtually controlled Skagway until he was killed in a shoot-out by the town surveyor and his gang was run out of town.

In the spring of 1898, the White Pass and Yukon Route railroad began construction as a saner and safer method of reaching the gold fields. An extraordinary and expensive piece of engineering, the completion of the 110-mile long railroad in 1900 came after the gold rush had peaked, but it helped Skagway survive by making the town a transportation center.

Even as early as 1899, as Skagway's population dwindled, residents tried to appeal to tourists, recognizing that the town represented something remarkable. Businessmen moved some of the town's most illustrious buildings to line Broadway Street, which was bisected by the railroad tracks. This shift changed the town's entire orientation from east-west to north-south.

Several entrepreneurs, including Skagway Street Car owner Martin Itjen and hotel owner Harriet Pullen, capitalized on the visitors who promenaded up the Inside Passage on steamer cruises. But when World War II killed the tourism market, Skagway fell dormant, relying largely on the railroad to survive. The wonderful old buildings on Broadway slumped

You'll think you stepped back in time when you visit Skagway.

into neglect. Remarkably, fire never swept the town, as it has in so many Alaska communities.

In 1977, the National Park Service rode to the rescue. With the creation of the Klondike Gold Rush National Historical Park (a companion segment is located in Seattle), the agency bought and restored many important Skagway buildings to their previous splendor, even down to the proper paint colors and wallpaper designs. Merchants lease space in the structures. Private owners also fixed up their property, and new buildings were constructed to fit in with the frontier Victorian style. The restoration project continues today, but this revival of history has made Skagway one of the most picturesque and interesting of Southeast ports. (The producers of the hit television series *Northern Exposure* reportedly considered filming the show in Skagway because it had the right look for the mythical town of Cicely, but the cost was prohibitive.)

Attractions

From the moment ferries and cruise ships dock at the site of wharves that once reached out to Klondikers, passengers are in the grip of history. A short walk away is the Klondike Gold Rush National Historical Park Visitor Center, housed in the restored White Pass and Yukon Route railroad depot and administration building at the entrance to Broadway Street. Historical displays detail the gold rush drama, and staff and brochures explain Skagway's present attractions.

Next to the park headquarters is the modern railway depot, where trains chug into the station. It's hard to resist the lure of the lonesome whistle and clanging bells as the train huffs its way into town. The railroad offers daily three-hour trips along the narrow-gauge rails to the summit of White Pass, viewing such landmarks as Bridal Veil and Pitchfork falls and the infamous Dead Horse Gulch, where 3,000 pack animals died from overwork.

On west 2nd Avenue, take a peek at Jeff Smith's Parlor, where the con artist conducted his shenanigans. The building was moved here in 1964 from its 6th Avenue locale. The building's original front remains intact and dates to 1898. It is privately owned.

Across from the parlor is the Red Onion Saloon. The stuffed floozy in

101

the window clues you in to its original purpose as a bawdy house and bar. The structure was built in 1897 at a different location, using planks from Capt. Moore's sawmill. When the building was later dragged to its current site, it was turned backwards, requiring a new entrance.

The saloon downstairs satisfied the customers' thirst, and the brothel upstairs satisfied their desires. The girls, wearing colorful names and little else, plied their trade in 10 tiny cubicles. Customers paid by dropping the fee, usually $1 to $5, through slots in the room's floor leading to the bartender. Clients could tell when certain women were busy; dolls representing each sporting lady were propped up or laid down, depending on her current status.

The saloon was reopened in 1980 with many original fittings, including the bar. It also seems to have retained a resident ghost who reportedly doesn't care much for men. Today, the joint is popular with visitors and residents alike, especially when musicians from the cruise ships drop in to jam.

You can't miss the Arctic Brotherhood Hall between 2nd and 3rd avenues. It's the building covered with more than 20,000 pieces of driftwood formed into designs and mosaics in a style called "rustic Victorian." Look below the flagpole to see the organization's logo, a gold pan with the initials AB.

The Arctic Brotherhood was a fraternal organization formed in 1899 in Skagway and later spread to more than 30 such camps in Alaska, Yukon and British Columbia. Following the induction of the last member—President Warren G. Harding, who joined during his 1923 visit to Alaska—the organization died. The building today houses the town's visitor information center, open daily. Ask for the free walking tour brochure, *Footsteps Into the Land of Gold*.

Down the street at 3rd and Broadway is the Mascot Saloon, restored by the park service. The original "Mascotte" Saloon opened in 1898 and was one of 80 such establishments in town before a stiff licensing fee slashed their numbers. During the height of the rush, prospectors flopped on the floor here for some shut-eye. The re-created saloon scene portrays the saloon in about 1910. Three model drinkers perpetually hoist their drinks at the stand-up bar. "I thought they were real people," remarked one startled visitor, peering into the saloon. Another tourist, spotting the replica bottles lined up behind the bar and in the window, asked, "Can you buy liquor by

The restored offices of the White Pass & Yukon Route house the Klondike Gold Rush National Historical Park Museum in Skagway.

the bottle here?" The ranger directed her down the street to a real liquor store. Display cases in the saloon exhibit a few of the more than 19,000 artifacts excavated in 1986 from beneath the building, including poker chips and dice, saloon tokens, and a rifle cartridge.

Across the street, the Golden North Hotel is adorned with a distinctive onion dome, an advertising gimmick meant to be spotted by incoming ship passengers. Rooms are furnished with period furniture from Skagway homes. The modern owners claim that a ghost, "Mary," lives in room 24, wearing a wedding dress and forever waiting for her fiancé to return from the gold fields. Local residents in the know say the story is more fiction than fact.

The large Lynch and Kennedy building between 3rd and 4th avenues was once a dry goods store catering mostly to men. The park service is restoring the structure. Also on the list of restorations is the Pantheon Saloon across the street.

Kirmse's Jewelry and Curio Store at 5th and Broadway displays two chains of gold nuggets claimed to be the largest and smallest in the world. Both chains were crafted by Herman Kirmse in 1898, shortly after he established his store. Also on display is the Colt .41 said to belong to Soapy Smith.

Among the cluster of gift shops and cafes on Broadway, look for Dedman's Photo Shop and its collection of historical postcards and photographs, many dating from 1898. The store was formed from two shacks joined by a false front and has a venerable history as the former studio of photographer E.A. Hegg, who documented many northern gold rushes.

This is now the oldest family business in town, owned by Barbara Dedman Kalen, the granddaughter of one of Skagway's early pioneers. Her parents snapped hundreds of photographs of Skagway scenes and sold them on postcards. Take a seat next to the cash register and peruse the 20 or so binders filled with historic and contemporary scenes of Skagway and elsewhere.

In the 5th Avenue block of Spring Street is where it all began. The cabin and home belonging to the Moore family still stand here on a grassy lot. (Some of the cabin's logs have been replaced, but old newspapers still line the walls inside.) The White Pass trail began on this lot. After Moore sold his wharf to the White Pass railway, he built a mansion before retiring to Victoria, B.C.

Look at the unassuming Peniel Mission on 6th Avenue for an example of how time treated Skagway's old buildings. A missionary from an evangelical but non-denominational sect arrived from Juneau in 1898, wearing a sailor hat with the words "Peniel Mission" on the band and carrying only $8. Two years later, local subscriptions paid for the gospel hall, where missionary women lived upstairs until about 1920. Archaeologists retrieved more than 38,000 artifacts from two seasons' excavation of a dump near the mission. The items help explain what people wore, ate and drank during this exciting period in Alaska history. The park service plans to restore the mission.

The nearby Molly Walsh Park celebrates the memory of another woman who touched Skagway history. During the gold rush, Molly married packer Mike Bartlett and followed him to Nome, but later, unhappy and lonely, ran away with his partner. Her husband followed her to Seattle and shot her dead. But Packer Jack Newman had loved Molly before Bartlett did, and he mooned over her memory so much that he eventually commissioned this bust of her, to the annoyance of his wife. Look closely at Molly's throat; the cameo there bears the profile of lovelorn Packer Jack.

Down the block and across the creek is the site where Harriet "Ma" Pullen opened her famous hotel in the Moore mansion, which she leased in 1901 and later bought. Only the stone chimney of this establishment remains standing in the meadow. The decaying building was demolished recently as a hazard.

Ma Pullen was proof that many of the women drawn into the Klondike Rush had just as much grit and gumption as the men. She came by steamer to Skagway in 1897 with just a few dollars, but by cooking in the day and baking dried apple pies in pans hammered from tin cans at night, she soon bought a cabin and sent for her family. Later she hauled supplies over the White Pass. When she opened her hotel, her reputation flowered as Alaska's premier hostess. Guests enjoyed cream from her cows, rode in her horse-drawn coach, and admired her gold rush memorabilia. President Harding once gave a speech from the porch. Ma Pullen died in 1947, with the hotel surviving her only another decade.

You can see some of her belongings in the Trail of '98 Museum. The museum is housed on the second floor of the old McCabe College building on 7th Avenue, now home to City Hall. The museum is a delightful collection of artifacts and memorabilia, many of them donated by Skagway families. Here you can learn more about Harriet Pullen's fellow characters, including Capt. Moore, Soapy Smith, Martin Itjen and other luminaries. (The tie in the Soapy Smith exhibit is said to be the one he wore when he was shot.) Gambling equipment from local saloons, a room decorated with Victorian furnishings, and items carried by stampeders depict Skagway's colorful history.

Be sure to spend a few moments reading from the documents displayed under glass. They range from *The Skagway Police Gazette* of 1909, billed as a "spasmodic publication," to a search warrant for chickens stolen from a Mrs. Achison in 1920. Also amusing is the petition from a resident asking the Skagway Council to regulate free-running livestock in the city, two offending goats in particular.

Though Skagway's history is neatly gathered up in the downtown district, other sites in the area tell more of the story. The Gold Rush

Cemetery, a mile-and-a-half beyond town, offers mute testimony to the varied lives whose fates became entwined with that of Skagway. Simple markers memorialize a murdered honeymoon couple, young children struck down by disease, a strangled lady of the evening, and a mother killed in childbirth. Frank Reid and Soapy Smith are buried here as well. An interesting guidebook to the cemetery is sold at the Trail of '98 Museum.

A couple of times a week, park rangers lead tours at Dyea town site, about nine miles from Skagway. Little can be seen of Skagway's rival today except the wharf and some ruins. Along the way are vistas of Long Bay and the Slide Cemetery, where three-score victims of a tragic 1898 avalanche on the Chilkoot Trail are buried. You'll also pass the infamous pass itself.

It's not possible to travel the White Pass on foot, but the Klondike Highway No. 2 and the WP&YR train parallel much of the trail. Imagine trekking up this pass in the cold and deep snows of winter not once, but many times, while carrying impossibly heavy burdens. Every stampeder was required by Canada to enter with a ton of supplies. It was said that even the horses occasionally jumped off cliffs to relieve their misery. Turnouts and interpretive signs along the highway point out significant spots. Canada Customs is located at Mile 22.2.

Once the Gold Rush faded, Skagway relied on a series of boomlets for survival. World War II curtailed tourism but caused an invasion of 12,000 troops into Skagway. In decades after the war, tourism and transportation again became the town's economic lifelines. The railway transported lead, zinc, and copper ore from Yukon mines until an economic depression shut it down in 1982, a disaster for Skagway employees. Skagway held on, though, sustained by growing tourism, and the railroad reopened in 1988 for summertime excursions. After years of periodic construction, Klondike Highway No. 2 finally opened year-round in 1986, linking Skagway with Whitehorse and the Alaska Highway.

Visitor Information

The Klondike Gold Rush National Historical Park has a visitor center at 2nd Avenue and Broadway Street, open daily from 8 a.m. to 6 p.m. The center includes historical displays, films, lectures, brochures, and ranger talks. Walking tours of the eight-block historical district leave from the

106

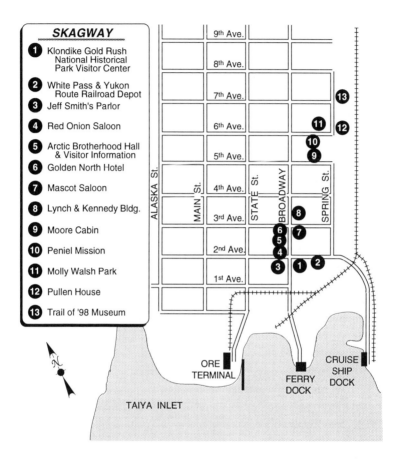

SKAGWAY

1. Klondike Gold Rush National Historical Park Visitor Center
2. White Pass & Yukon Route Railroad Depot
3. Jeff Smith's Parlor
4. Red Onion Saloon
5. Arctic Brotherhood Hall & Visitor Information
6. Golden North Hotel
7. Mascot Saloon
8. Lynch & Kennedy Bldg.
9. Moore Cabin
10. Peniel Mission
11. Molly Walsh Park
12. Pullen House
13. Trail of '98 Museum

lobby at 11 a.m. and 3 p.m. Check the bulletin board for information about Dyea tours. The center also includes Chilkoot Pass trail information and a list of approved guide services. The park encompasses units at Dyea, Chilkoot Trail, White Pass Trail and Seattle. Write to: Superintendent, P.O. Box 517, Skagway, 99840. Call 983-2921.

Arctic Brotherhood Hall on Broadway Street houses the visitor information center, open daily from 8 a.m. to 5 p.m. Brochures and other information are available. A half-hour film, *The Skagway Story*, is screened daily for a small admission fee. Write to the Skagway Convention and Visitors Bureau at P.O. Box 415, Skagway, 99840. Call 983-2908.

The Skagway News Co. publishes an excellent free guide to Skagway history and services, distributed on the state ferry and elsewhere. Write to: Box 1898, Skagway, 99840. Call 983-2354.

Folks with gold stampeders for relatives can join the Klondike Stampeders Relatives Association by writing to: P.O. Box 325, Skagway, 99840.

Transportation

Skagway remains an important transportation link, with connections by sea, air, highway, and rail. The state ferry docks about a third of a mile from downtown Skagway, making walking easy. Many inns and hotels offer courtesy transportation; taxi service is available. The ferry terminal number is 983-2941.

Skagway is a popular stop with cruise ships, which dock at the harbor within walking distance of downtown. At the docks you may see freighters loading ore or timber from Canada.

Water taxi service to Haines is scheduled daily in the mornings. The M/V *Fairweather* travels between Juneau and Skagway.

Jets do not stop at Skagway, but several small flight services offer charter and scheduled service to other communities. The airstrip is a few blocks from downtown Skagway, just past Alaska Street. Flight services and hotels offer courtesy rides.

The White Pass and Yukon Route railway connects Skagway with Fraser, B.C., with motor-coach transfers to Whitehorse. The railway also picks up Chilkoot Pass hikers and carries passengers on round-trip excursions to White Pass Summit. Call 1-800-478-7373 outside of Alaska, or 983-2217 within Alaska. Write: P.O. Box 435, Skagway, 99840. The rail depot is on 2nd Avenue.

Car rentals are available in town. Motorcoaches and vans transport passengers daily to Haines, Whitehorse, Fairbanks and Anchorage.

Accommodations

Rooms are available at several historic or modern hotels, lodges, bed-and-breakfast inns, and a bunkhouse. Motorcoach tours are liable to book up some establishments, so reservations are advisable. For a complete list of hostelries and other businesses, contact the Skagway Convention and

Visitors Bureau and ask for the list of accommodations and services.

Recreational vehicles can choose from among Pullen Creek RV Park, near the ferry terminal; Hanousek Park Campground, in a wooded area at 12th and Broadway; Hoover's, downtown at 4th and State; and Liarsville, about 2.5 miles from town.

Tent camping is available at the Hanousek and Liarsville campgrounds. Also, a public campground, operated by the National Park Service, is open at Dyea, but facilities are limited.

The Skagway Home Hostel is located in a historic home at 3rd Street near Main, a half-mile from the airport and a half-mile from the ferry. Registration is from 5 p.m. to 10:30 p.m. Late ferry arrivals are accommodated. With just 15 beds available, reservations are advised. Call 983-2131 or write: Box 231, Skagway, 99840.

Eateries include fast food, cafes, sidewalk stands, and fine dining.

Entertainment

The Days of '98 Show, a musical melodrama featuring dance hall girls, ragtime music, and Soapy Smith, is staged daily at the Eagles Dance Hall, 6th and Broadway. Check the marquee for times or call 983-2545. Tickets are sold at the box office. The evening performance includes time to gamble at roulette, cards and dice for souvenir prizes.

The dramatic rhymes of the Bard of the North, Robert Service, are performed with great flourish by "Buckwheat," who also tells tall tales. Nightly performances are scheduled at the Arctic Brotherhood Hall. Tickets are available at the door.

On downtown streets you can amuse yourself by posing in vintage costumes for portraits, panning for gold and shopping for souvenirs and art in the numerous galleries and shops.

Excursions

For such a small town, you'll have a wide choice of tour vehicles. Some enjoy the nostalgic street cars and trolleys, while others prefer contemporary taxis or buses. Tours available include town highlights, the Burro Creek salmon hatchery, Dyea, and the Gold Rush Cemetery. Check with the visitor center.

Flightseeing tours of the Juneau Ice Cap, Glacier Bay, Haines' Chilkat Valley, or gold rush trails can be arranged by plane or helicopter. Contact the visitor center or a travel agent.

The White Pass and Yukon Route railway chugs along a narrow-gauge track to the summit of White Pass and back twice a day. Call 983-2217 or stop at the depot on 2nd Ave.

Events

Skagway residents make the most of Independence Day, following the lead of Soapy Smith, who rode a white horse in the town's first Fourth of July celebration in 1898. Count yourself lucky if you're in town to see Skagway's parade, for it's considered one of the liveliest in Alaska. Since just about everybody in town seems to be in the parade, they need visitors to be the spectators anyway.

Soapy Smith's Wake, held at the Gold Rush Cemetery, commemorates his death on July 8. If his great-grandson doesn't attend, he sends money for champagne.

In March, residents break the cabin fever blues with the Windfest, which features an ugly dog contest, chain saw toss and ore truck pull among its unusual events. It's almost worth making a trip to Alaska in the winter.

Outdoor Recreation

The most famous trail in Alaska history is Chilkoot Pass, 33 miles of heartbreak and toil for the Klondikers who struggled up it almost a century ago. The trail still draws many who want to test themselves on a four-to five-day mountain trek through history over the summit at 3,700 feet and on to Lake Bennett.

The trailhead begins at about Mile 7 Dyea Road. The trail offers several shelters and campsites, but it should not be underestimated. Careful planning is a must. Information about approved guide services, suggested equipment, trail conditions and the hike itself is available from the National Park Service headquarters on Broadway St. Many hikers return to Skagway on the White Pass railway by taking a track car from Lake Bennett to Fraser. Check with the train office for details.

Good hiking can be found on other trails in the area as well. Ask for the *Skagway and Vicinity Hiking Trails* brochure from the visitor center. The Dewey Lake Trails System includes several paths ranging from easy to challenging. The trails begin across the rail tracks at the end of 3rd Avenue. Upper and Lower Dewey lakes tease anglers with brook trout.

Yakutania Point Park offers views of the head of Lynn Canal and facilities for picnicking. You can walk to the park by heading toward the airport runway along 1st Avenue. Cross the Skagway River footbridge and turn left to the park. Turn right and you'll encounter the local Pet Cemetery, where some graves date back 30 years or more.

Pullen Creek Park and Molly Walsh Park downtown also have picnic facilities.

Soapy Smith

Entire books have been written about the rogue's life led by Jefferson "Soapy" Smith, but his end on July 8, 1898, was summed up most succinctly by this headline in the *Skaguay News*: "Dead in a Moment—Shot Through Heart."

Soapy lived as he had died—with great drama and flair. His career as a con man began long before he arrived in Skagway in fall 1897 with five colleagues in crime, but in the wild-hearted town he flourished. Likable, smooth and gentlemanly, with a dapper bearing and upstanding manner that belied his dark intentions, he established a crime syndicate so far-reaching that nobody in town could be sure who was in cahoots with him.

Soapy Smith's prime rule was to never fleece permanent residents, only transients. One of his most famous scams was a telegraph office, where people could pay $5 to send a message anywhere in the world. Somehow, the message-senders never noticed there were no telegraph lines in Skagway.

Smith and his henchmen soon controlled the docks, the streets and the trails. He opened his own saloon in a small building now on Second Avenue. But Smith had a taste for glory as well. When the Spanish-American War broke out in 1898, he whipped up patriotic fervor and formed a volunteer militia. The militia conveniently served as a prime opportunity to unload soldiers of their valuables while they were examined by a fake doctor. In the Fourth of July parade, he rode at the head of this guard.

When a hapless prospector named J.D. Stewart was relieved of his $2,000 gold poke, a local vigilante committee demanded the return of the gold. On the evening of July 8, as citizens met on the town's Juneau Wharf

The grateful citizens of Skagway erected this memorial to Frank Reid who died from wounds sustained in a shootout with Soapy Smith.

to discuss how to run the gang out, Smith appeared with a Winchester rifle in his hand and a derringer and Colt .45 on his person and approached a group of men guarding the dock's entrance. One of the men was town surveyor Frank Reid.

After the two men exchanged sharp words, Smith held the muzzle of his rifle to Reid's head. Reid shoved the muzzle down and drew his six-gun. "My God, don't shoot!" Smith cried, but as Reid's gun misfired, Smith shot the surveyor in the groin. Each fired again; this time Reid's bullet pierced Smith's heart, killing him instantly. Reid, now wounded in the knee, collapsed. "I'm badly hurt boys, but I got him first," he said. Twelve days of agony later, Reid died. His funeral was Skagway's largest, and grateful citizens erected a stone monument that said, "He gave his life for the honor of Skagway."

As for Soapy, he was buried six feet outside the cemetery's boundary with a plain wood marker (later replaced). The Presbyterian preacher who buried him chose as the text, "The Way of Transgressors is Hard." Soapy surely would be pleased to see how the legend of his life has not only persisted, but flourished, for it seems everyone loves a bad guy. A wake is held on the anniversary of his death, thanks to the sponsorship of his great-grandson in California. The tale making the rounds in 1992 was that wake participants ended their revelry by urinating on Reid's monument. Officials sent them back the next day with scrub brushes to make amends.

Gustavus and Glacier Bay

Few places in Alaska excite the imagination like Glacier Bay NationalPark and Preserve. Even in a state where beauty stretches beyond the horizon wherever you look, Glacier Bay National Park and Preserve offers a concentrated dose of Alaska. It would seem enough to encounter either the thunderous roar of calving glaciers, the spectacular acrobatics of humpback whales, or the ice-bound heights of the lofty Fairweather and St. Elias mountain ranges, but here the visitor is likely to enjoy all three, and more.

So it seems almost ironic that the neighboring community of Gustavus is so, well, modest. And quiet. "I can't believe how quiet it is here," one visitor marveled. After the evening jet has departed for Juneau, it seems so tranquil you can almost hear the vegetables and flowers growing through the long summer evenings.

That's the way the 200 or so residents of Gustavus like it. Not even the state ferries stop here. Visitors cruising into Glacier Bay may hardly notice the tiny rural community spread across the glacial flats 10 miles from the park boundary. Those driving from the Gustavus airport to Bartlett Cove might miss the town itself if they blink. That would be a shame, because you'll not find a more pastoral, peaceful community in Southeast Alaska.

Unlike most of Southeast's settlements, Gustavus inhabits entirely flat land, left behind courtesy of glacial retreat. The homesteaders who arrived in 1914 figured the area for a likely farming spot. Despite early setbacks, settlers found the rich sedge fields ideal for raising cattle and produce. Originally known as Strawberry Point for the luscious wild strawberries filling the meadows, the town eventually adopted the name of nearby Point

Gustavus, so christened for the King of Sweden.

Early homesteaders contended with grizzly bears that tended to regard cattle as hamburger on the hoof. Gustavus' modern gardeners are learning to deal with new neighbors — moose, which recently have begun migrating into the area. Bears still wander through to munch on strawberries and, later in the season, to fill up on salmon swimming up Salmon River.

Prospectors searched for gold in the region as well. A few legendary characters spent their entire lives seeking fortunes along the inlets and mountainsides. An independent lot, they also battled the government when it restricted mining in 1925 by declaring Glacier Bay a national monument. The miners convinced the government to reopen the area for claim staking.

Among these warriors was Joe Ibach. If you cruise by Reid Inlet, ask the park naturalist on board to point out Joe and Muz Ibach's rustic cabin near the waterway's entrance. Though they never made a fortune prospecting, their life together must have been rich. They agreed if one of them died, the other would follow right away. Muz passed away in Juneau in 1959, and Joe shot himself the next year, remarking in his will that, "There's a time to live and a time to die. This is the time."

Long before the Ibachs and their colleagues arrived, aboriginal people lived here. Archaeological investigation has uncovered 10,000-year-old sites nearby. Tlingit oral history indicates that the Little Ice Age about 4,000 years ago forced people from "Tcukanedit," or "Valley of the River of Grass," to the village of Hoonah on Chichagof Island, 20 miles from the bay's entrance. The Native legend says that a young girl confined during puberty called down the ice that drove the people out.

Today, cable TV, satellite dishes and espresso have found their way to Gustavus, but little else has. Bicycles outrank motor vehicles as a favored method of transportation along the dirt roads. If you want any dry-cleaning done, send it by small plane to Juneau. Scattered along the roads and through the meadows are farms, houses, a post office, a mercantile, a few galleries and souvenir shops, an airstrip, a school, and a library. ("All three books are on reserve," joke park bus drivers.) Good food is a given, with meals based on harvests from gardens and the sea.

In short, Gustavus is about as rural as it gets in Southeast Alaska. Residents casually mention that most homes now have electricity, or complain that newcomers expect immediate cable hookup. Things are supposed to be slow here, after all. The sleepy Salmon River, meandering into Icy Strait with little fanfare, seems made for casting a line. The town news is collected in a monthly four-page newsletter, the Strawberry Point Chronicle, where the front-page article might be a plea for drivers to slow down and walkers to clear out of the middle of the road. Residents aren't much interested in city government; they run things with a community association and volunteer emergency services.

In summer not only visitors but part-time residents swell the population. Many homesteading families, having long ago paid their dues, spend their winters in gentler climes but return to Gustavus for the warm months. The presence of a real estate office testifies to the recent trend of breaking up 160-acre homestead parcels into house or cabin lots, enticing residents of other communities to summer here. Year-round jobs are scarce, with many permanent residents earning a living from seasonal work in tourism or fishing.

Though Gustavus' laid-back style is attraction enough for those seeking a wilderness retreat, most people come, of course, to see the wonders of Glacier Bay. One of the earliest was naturalist John Muir, who explored the bay by canoe in 1879 and wrote about his experiences in *Travels in Alaska*. He was soon followed by steamship cruises carrying awed tourists.

In 1925, advocates of the park's treasures persuaded President Calvin Coolidge to create Glacier Bay National Monument. In later years the boundaries expanded and contracted, until by 1980, the area became Glacier Bay National Park and Preserve, with 3.2 million acres protected in the park and an additional 57,000 acres designated as national preserve. Nearly half of Alaska's tidewater glaciers are sheltered in the inlets and arms of the park, their snouts nudging into the water. A dozen of the 16 tidewater glaciers here stage theatrical displays of calving, shedding enormous cascades of ice into the water and choking inlets with slush and icebergs.

Gliding past the mountain peaks, fjords and glaciers, it's hard to believe that 200 years ago this bay did not exist. In 1794, when Capt. George Vancouver explored this region as part of his journey through Southeast Alaska, he saw only a massive wall of ice stretching 20 miles or more. But less than a century later, when naturalist John Muir explored the region, 48 miles of the bay had been exposed inland by retreating ice. The retreat's incredible pace has slowed recently, though some glaciers temporarily advance at times. John Muir Glacier, for example, was some seven miles closer just 30 years ago.

Like Muir Glacier, many of the glaciers are named for early adventurers and scientists who surveyed the bay. Today, the park remains a scientific Mecca for glaciologists, naturalists and other researchers seeking to understand not only more about glaciers but about how the land revegetates in a process called succession. Park naturalists who accompany cruise tours into the bay can explain more about the geological and biological dynamics.

Competing with the glaciers for attention are the St. Elias and Fairweather ranges ringing the park, forever grasped by winter and grazing the sky with peaks reaching from 12,000 to 15,000 feet high. Mount Fairweather, at 15,320 feet, is taller than any peak in the other 49 states.

Though it may be difficult to tear your eyes from the scenery, look around at the abundant wildlife. The landscape may appear barren in places, particularly in the upper inlets near the glaciers, but as vegetation and forests repopulate, so do the creatures. More than 200 species of nesting or migrating birds have been identified in the park. Colonies of black-legged kittiwakes perch impossibly along the sheer cliffs. Arctic terns fly from Antarctica to Glacier Bay to nest along these shores, while phalaropes commute from South America. Orange-billed oystercatchers, crying shrilly, skitter along the rocks. The comical tufted and horned puffins always thrill viewers.

Every visitor hopes to see the fabled community of humpback whales that summer in the bay and nearby Icy Strait. (They winter in Hawaii and other warm spots; not a bad life, eh?) From late June through August, as many as two dozen whales feed on schooling fish, tiny crustaceans and other organisms in the bay. Researchers have dubbed returning whales with names like Frenchie, Gertrude, Garfuncle and Max.

In the 1980s, concern about the possible effect of vessel traffic on the whales prompted the park service to limit the number of boats entering the bay each season. Even pleasure motorboats need permits to travel within the park.

In these waters you may also encounter orcas, or killer whales, minke whales, Dall and harbor porpoises, and sea lions. A real treat is to see harbor seals hauled out on icebergs, where the young are pupped. A biologist once counted as many as 3,500 seals in Johns Hopkins Inlet

Glacier Bay is a high point for many cruise ship passengers.

alone. Seals also congregate in Muir Inlet in large numbers, possibly to avoid killer whales, which don't enter the inlet's upper waters.

Scan cliffs for the telltale white spots indicating mountain goats. You may spot black or brown bears grazing along the shorelines. Red fox, deer, porcupines, lynx, coyotes and other small mammals also live here. Since about midcentury, moose have been spotted in ever-increasing numbers as they apparently migrate from Lynn Canal and spread throughout the park. On rare occasions, fortunate visitors may glimpse wolves.

Many of Glacier Bay's wonders will never be seen by the casual traveler, but they deserve mention so that no one goes home believing they have seen it all. One such place is Lituya Bay on the park's outer coast. The deep bay is notorious for its hazardous entrance, which claimed the lives of 21 crewmen of French explorer Jean de La Perouse in 1786. Several times in past centuries, earthquakes have jolted loose enormous landslides into the bay, creating incredible tidal waves that swept the bay. The most recent, in July 10, 1958, wiped out one fishing boat and its crew, and nearly took the lives of others anchored in the bay.

The Dry Bay area is a little-known wilderness added to park boundaries in 1980. In landscape even more remote than Glacier Bay, the Alsek River completes its tumultuous journey from Canada by emptying into the bay on the gulf coast, near Yakutat. The river, which is fed by the mighty Tatshenshini River, is a major route for adventure rafters. Guided trips are available from Alaska outfitters.

Visitor Information

The Gustavus Visitors Association offers a map and list of accommodations, services, restaurants, stores, and other information. Write to: PO. Box 167, Gustavus, 99826. There is no visitor center in the town itself, but you'll find residents helpful.

The National Park Service distributes information about excursions, services, camping, boating, permits and regulations at its visitor center inside Glacier Bay Lodge and at its information station near Bartlett Cove dock. Write to: Superintendent, Glacier Bay National Park and Preserve, Gustavus, 99826, or call (907) 697-2230.

The park service visitor center on the upper floor of Glacier Bay Lodge displays films, evening programs, natural history exhibits and other information. The Alaska Natural History Association sells maps, nautical charts and other publications here, including an official park handbook, *Glacier Bay*.

Transportation

State ferries don't visit Gustavus, but jets do. Gustavus is a short hop away from Juneau, 65 miles to the west. Several air taxis offer scheduled and charter service as well.

Gustavus is a major destination on the itinerary of several cruise ship lines traveling the Inside Passage. From Juneau or Gustavus it is possible to arrange specialty cruises into the park that last anywhere from a day to overnight to a week. Ask your travel agent or check with the Juneau or Gustavus visitor associations.

Once in Gustavus, most inns offer guests courtesy transportation to and from the airstrip. Many have bikes available to clients and others. Bartlett Cove and Glacier Bay Lodge are 10 miles by road from Gustavus.

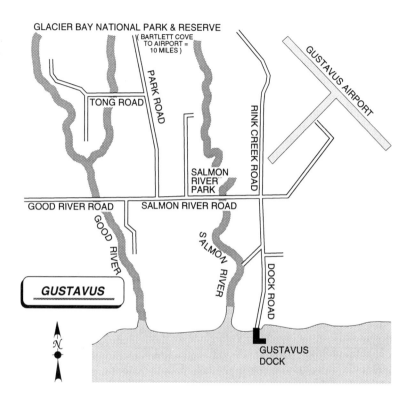

Glacier Bay Lodge has free bus rides for customers but charges several dollars for non-clients. Ask the driver. A taxi service is on call as well.

Accommodations

The community offers several inns, cabins, and bed and breakfast establishments. The famous Gustavus Inn, a former homestead, is rightly heralded for its excellent fare and cozy accommodations, but you'll need reservations even to lunch here. Don't despair; other establishments also offer homemade baking, local seafood and produce, and comfortable lodgings. Check with the visitor association.

Glacier Bay Lodge, open only during the visitor season, is the sole private concessionaire inside the park. Located at Bartlett Cove, 10 miles from Gustavus, the lodge has 55 rooms and 26 less-expensive dorm rooms. A restaurant, gift shop, fuel dock and cruise ships are available. Kayak rentals, charter fishing and sightseeing package tours can be arranged at the lodge. Call 1-800-451-5952 or contact travel agents.

A free park campground with 25 sites is located at Bartlett Cove just a short hike from the lodge. Bear-resistant food caches, firewood, and a warming hut are available.

The lodge's comfortable fittings may lull you into forgetting you're in the Alaskan wilderness. Stroll along the nearby paths, and the bear droppings dotting the trails will quickly dispense with that illusion. Bear encounters are always a possibility here. Lodge staff have a rule of thumb for anyone who comes face-to-face with a bruin: "If you run, you're done." Read the National Park Service's newsletter for tips on living peacefully with the local bears.

Excursions

Charters focusing on whale-watching, fishing, or glacier-viewing may be arranged in Gustavus, Juneau, or at the park lodge.

If you don't have much time, consider a flightseeing trip for at least an overview of the mountains and glaciers. Check with air taxis in Juneau, Skagway, Haines, or Gustavus for tour information.

Independent travelers enjoy not only fishing but kayaking, backcountry hiking, and wildlife photography. Many Gustavus residents make their living guiding visitors to the park's delights. Ask for the list of services from the Gustavus Visitors Association, or check with a travel agent.

Outdoor Recreation

Some visitors prefer to explore Glacier Bay's wilderness on their own, often by kayak. They are well-advised to take advantage of park service information and expertise before setting out. Like much of Alaska, the beauty here is accompanied by an equal dose of danger. Calving glaciers can swamp kayaks; bears can wander through campsites; bad weather can turn a fun trip into a fatal one.

Conversely, regulations and permits protect the park from humans.

Though backcountry permits are not required, they are recommended. Power-boaters must obtain vessel permits before entering Bartlett Cove or Glacier Bay.

Park service rangers give daily camper orientations at the lodge to convey important information about backcountry practices and regulations. A map at the information station near Bartlett Cove dock marks areas closed because of bear activity or bird nesting. Though only two campers have been killed in the past quarter-century in the park, each year there are an average of 15 camper/bear incidents. Check out the ranger station's display of bear-chewed camping gear for some sobering insight.

No established trails disturb the landscape in the upper bay, though hiking is possible along shores and up hills. Naturalists lead hikes on a three mile trail near Glacier Bay Lodge that winds through the forest to the estuary of Bartlett River. A mile-long forest trail begins at the lodge and ends at the dock. Strolls along the beach offer lovely vistas and close-ups of intertidal life.

Backcountry explorers generally require drop-offs and pick-ups by airplane or by the park's small tour boats. Check at the lodge for information. For hard-core paddlers, the state ferry does stop at Hoonah, 20 miles across Icy Strait.

Detailed kayaking and hiking requirements and routes are thoroughly covered in *Glacier Bay National Park: A Backcountry Guide to the Glaciers and Beyond*, by Jim DuFresne, published by The Mountaineers, 306 2nd Ave., W., Seattle, WA 98119. The official National Park Handbook also is jammed with general information, and is sold in the park service center at the lodge.

Byways and Eddies

S ay you're the kind of traveler who wants to go where everyone else is not going. Say you want to see the parts of Southeast where there are no T-shirt shops, no cruise ships, no crowds. Instead, you're looking for an easy pace, an intimacy with the land and sea, and people who value their independence. You can find all of that, and more, off the beaten track. Most of the time there isn't any track at all. Many of these villages have few or no formal tourist attractions, but then, that's why people like them.

Hyder

It's a good bet that most Alaskans think Hyder is in British Columbia. That's because Hyder is so close to the border it might as well be in British Columbia. Hyder residents even use a Canadian area code.

The confusion probably stems from Hyder's link by road and reputation with Stewart, B.C. Just two miles apart by road, the two towns are both busted gold towns. Both communities lie at the head of the 90-mile Portland Canal and both are connected by a 40-mile-long spur road with the Cassiar Highway, making Hyder one of three Southeast Alaska communities you can drive to. You can also hop on the state ferry *Aurora* in Ketchikan for a weekly visit. The ferry docks for a couple of hours, giving you plenty of time to look around what residents call the "friendliest ghost town in Alaska."

With just 80 or so residents, Hyder is also one of the tiniest towns in Alaska. There's nothing small about its scenery, though. From its perch at the canal's edge, the town looks up to a crown of mountains. Nearby tours based in Stewart include trips to the Salmon Glacier Ice Fields, lakes, streams, and old mining sites. Stewart has just over 2,000 residents, and between the two neighbors you'll have no problem finding motels, restaurants, stores, or campgrounds. Hyder even has its own walking tour map, available from the Canal Trading Post.

For more information, write the Stewart Historical Society at: Box 402, Stewart, BC V0T 1W0, or call the Hyder Community Association at: (604) 636-2498.

Metlakatla

Metlakatla has a history like no other town in Southeast. The community was established in 1887 on Annette Island, just 15 miles south of Ketchikan. Most of the 1,400 residents are Tsimshian Indian. Their ancestors originally migrated here from near Prince Rupert, B.C., under the leadership of Father William Duncan, an Anglican lay priest who split from the church and led his flock by canoe to the Metlakatla site on Annette Island. The people built homes, a sawmill, and salmon cannery to sustain themselves, and Duncan persuaded the federal government to award the community reservation status. Metlakatla remains the only federal reservation in the state, but the Metlakatla Indian Community runs the town's affairs.

Several other aspects of Metlakatla distinguish it from the rest of Alaska. Because it is a reservation, fish traps are legal here. Elsewhere, the salmon traps were outlawed with statehood. Also, Metlakatla aligns with the Pacific Standard time zone, which the rest of Southeast briefly flirted with before returning to Alaska time. But because Metlakatla doesn't participate in Daylight Savings Time, residents share the same clock as Ketchikan from April through October.

Town leaders are proud of the strides Metlakatla has made in recent years by adding paved streets, a swimming pool, and centers for children, teens and senior citizens, as well as numerous social services. The Tamgas Fish Hatchery, releasing 16 million to 20 million young salmon each year, is one of the largest in Southeast, and the mill and cannery still operate.

Air taxis and regular ferry service connect Metlakatla with Ketchikan. The two-hour ferry ride makes it a convenient day trip. The terminal is just over a mile from town; walk or call a taxi. Anyone planning to stay more than a day or so needs a visitor's permit, available at the city council chambers. Accommodations are limited, but cafes and stores exist. Call the mayor's office at 886-4868 for information. You'll find people most helpful and friendly.

Tsimshian culture differs in important ways from Tlingit and Haida traditions. Though Duncan encouraged the use of the native tongue, he frowned on customs he considered unchristian. Today village elders and legends preserved by an anthropologist are helping to lay a foundation for preserving Tsimshian culture. A new tribal long house near the downtown waterfront hosts tribal dances and programs, and displays carvings and crafts. It is open to the public. Visitors also may be interested in the Duncan Museum housed inside the patriarch's original home. The distinguished William Duncan Memorial Church is a replica of the original destroyed by fire in 1948.

Prince of Wales Island

Prince of Wales Island is the only place in Southeast where you can drive among communities. The third-largest island in the United States, much of it is crisscrossed by more than a thousand miles of logging roads. The roads have opened up a good part of the northern island for outdoor recreation, but the South Prince of Wales Wilderness remains remote and pristine. The island is still yielding its secrets, some of them underground. The El Capitan cave is not only the largest in Alaska but the deepest in the United States, with a depth of 598 feet. A Forest Service sponsored project to map caves and passages continues to add still more known caverns to the mid-1992 total of 160.

About 3,500 people live scattered among the island's communities and logging camps. The state ferry travels between Ketchikan and Hollis, which offers little to visitors except a starting point. From there, roads link Craig, Klawock, Thorne Bay, Hydaburg, Coffman Cove, Whale Pass, Labouchere Bay, and Naukati. The only airstrip is located at Klawock, but float planes visit Craig, Thorne Bay, and Hydaburg. Most visitor services are available in larger communities.

The road from Hollis to Klawock and Craig is paved, while the others are gravel. Expect big trucks, occasional delays, and rough patches. It's a good idea to take an extra spare tire. Also, remember that large tracts have been clear-cut on both public and private land, which is why the logging roads are there in the first place. You should find plenty of scenery anyway. Before embarking for the island, pick up a road map from the Ketchikan ranger district office.

An incorporated town with a population of about 750, Klawock is about 25 miles from Hollis. The town offers supplies, a couple of restaurants, rental cabins, an RV campground, guides for nearby hunting and fishing, transient moorage, and other services. A totem park features replica and original poles salvaged from an abandoned village. Write to the city government at: P.O. Box 113, Klawock, 99925.

Just six miles down the road, you'll find Craig, the largest town on the island. Craig is actually a two-island town, as it stretches across a causeway to Craig Island. Most basic services are available, including stores, restaurants, gas, transient moorage, and more. The town was named after Craig Millar, a salmon packer who established the community at what was once a temporary fishing village. Until 1912, the town was called Fish Egg until it was renamed after Craig. Commercial fishing and logging are big here, but the area's abundant sport fish and game are drawing more visitors. Write to the city at: P.O. Box 23, Craig, 99921.

Thorne Bay, about 60 miles from Hollis, was once known as the "biggest logging camp in the U.S." Today, private land ownership has built the town into one of Alaska's newest baby cities, incorporated in 1982. The town of about 600 overlooks Clarence Strait and Cleveland Peninsula. Canoeing, fishing, and camping along the Thorne River and bay are popular. Overnight accommodations, gas, charters, stores and an RV park are available. Write to the city at P.O. Box 19110, Thorne Bay, 99919.

Hydaburg overlooks Sukkwan Narrows, about 36 miles from Hollis by road. The community is a meld of three Haida villages formed in 1911 by descendants of those who had migrated from British Columbia two centuries ago. At about 450 residents, the town is the largest Haida settlement in Alaska. Fishing and a cannery support residents. Limited visitor services include lodging, a restaurant, gas, and supplies. A totem park displays restored Haida poles, some of them most unusual. Write to the city at: Box 49, Hydaburg, 99922.

Toward the island's northeast end is Coffman Cove, an independent logging camp with a population of about 186. Limited visitor facilities include gas, groceries and meals. If you're headed north toward the end of the road, you'll find groceries, gas and a lodge at Whale Pass, but neither Naukati nor Labouchere Bay offers services for travelers. However, campsites and picnic areas are scattered along the route; check with the Forest Service.

130

Kake

Some people swear that Kake owns some of Southeast's best views. It also possesses some of its most dramatic history. An exchange of murderous reprisals between a few of the fierce Kake Tlingits and Sitka residents in 1869 prompted the U.S. Navy to shell three Kake villages into obliteration. The tribe later moved to its present site on Kupreanof Island, about 40 air miles northwest of Petersburg.

The village of nearly 700 people, mostly Native, receives weekly visits from state ferries and scheduled air service from Juneau and Petersburg. The town has some facilities, including overnight accommodations, food, supplies, and public moorage, but visitors will have to entertain themselves. Looming over town is a totem pole that tops over 132 feet, claimed to be the tallest in the world. Kake commissioned the pole from Chilkat carvers, who exhibited it at Expo '70 in Japan before it was returned here. Subsistence food gathering, commercial fishing and processing and logging sustain the village. Write to the city at: Box 500, Kake, 99830.

Kayakers find Admiralty Island a true paradise for their sport.

Angoon and Admiralty Island

A ngoon's nearly 700 residents would probably just as soon have their village to themselves, but as the only town on Admiralty Island, that's pretty much a lost cause. Residents have bowed to the inevitable as lodges and guide services cater to visitors drawn to the area's wildlife and scenery, but the town remains firmly traditional and largely undeveloped. Only in recent years did it acquire its first stop sign.

Float planes visit from Juneau, 60 air miles away, by charter and scheduled service. The ferry visits Angoon twice weekly, docking about 3 miles from town. Killisnoo Island, across from the dock, was once a whaling station and now shelters private lodges and homes. Visitor services include a motel, bed-and-breakfast, restaurant, general store and public moorage. A Forest Service campground is located near the ferry terminal.

In 1978 Congress gave the island monument status, and two years later designated 95 percent of the monument as wilderness, a status that includes more restrictions on activities. The Admiralty Island National Monument was recently renamed Kotznoowoo Wilderness, honoring the Tlingit name, which means "Fortress of the Bears." Only the Mansfield Peninsula at the northern tip remains separate from wilderness designation.

The island is not entirely untouched, of course. Greens Creek Mining Co. operates a silver mine within the monument. Some people own cabins in hideaways like Funter Bay. Logging has taken place on some private and public lands. But Angoon remains the only permanent settlement, with its own lands. All else is as close to unadulterated wilderness as one could find in Southeast Alaska.

More brown bears than people live here now, with close to one bear for every one of the island's 1,500 square miles. There also are more bald eagles

133

on Admiralty than in the continental United States. Admiralty Island also embraces some of the biggest old-growth timber stands in Southeast Alaska.

Tlingit cultural traditions are strong in Angoon, despite such modern innovations as cable television. Many residents depend on commercial fishing, seasonal work and government subsidies for cash. Food-gathering from the ocean, the intertidal zone, and the forest remain critical. Residents have resisted such development as an airstrip, for fear that visiting hunters will increase demands on local game.

Angoon was the site of an early altercation between the whites and Tlingits. In 1882 the USS *Corwin* bombarded Angoon, burning most of the village homes following trouble caused when a trading ship refused to compensate the tribe for the accidental death of a village shaman. In 1973 the U.S. government made a $90,000 cash settlement. Villagers commemorated the tragedy on its centennial by dedicating a cultural center and totems.

Part of Admiralty's appeal is its wealth of recreational opportunities, besides fishing and hunting. The Forest Service maintains a couple dozen public cabins at lakes and inlets on the island. The Cross-Admiralty Canoe Route traverses a series of lakes and waterways. Kayakers explore deep inlets and harbors. Adventure services and charters based in Juneau offer guided trips throughout the island.

More and more visitors are learning of the wondrous opportunity to watch brown bears in their natural setting at Pack Creek, a wildlife sanctuary about 40 miles southwest of Juneau. Because the area is in danger of being loved to death, Forest Service managers recently imposed a permit system for observers. Pack Creek, homesteaded by the late Stan Price who lived unafraid among the bruins, is home to a group of brown bears habituated to human presence. That does not make them tame, however. Strict observance of viewing rules allows people to stand on a spit and watch bears go about their business as they feed on salmon and stroll through the intertidal meadow. A viewing tower up the creek provides an aerial vantage.

Pack Creek can be reached by float plane, charter boat or kayak expedition. A limit of 24 visitors per day is enforced, requiring both permits and advance reservations between July 10 and Aug. 25. Four spaces a day are set aside for last-minute reservations. Make reservations by calling or visiting the Forest Service Information Center in Juneau's Centennial Hall, 586-8751, or the Admiralty Island National Monument, 8461 Old Dairy Road.

Tenakee Springs

Tenakee Springs is one of the few communities in the country that claims to be car-free. Only a fuel truck and fire engine drive the town's one street, Tenakee Avenue. Everybody else walks, bikes or rides all-terrain vehicles. People haul water and use outhouses because there is no water or sewer system. The local joke is "Come to Tenakee, set your watch back 30 years."

But that's why people live here, and that's why others come to visit this island idyll. Many of its 125 residents are retirees or drop-outs from the demands of modern life. It's the sort of place where people run a tab at the mercantile and consider themselves one big family. The tiny town also is a favorite get-away for folks living in larger cities, some who have summer homes. Here you can slip off the reins of civilization, wander the shoreline, soak in the springs, and relax.

It is the hot springs that are the big draw. After Natives pointed out the sulfur springs to whites, miners from Juneau and Sitka, and eventually the Yukon and Interior Alaska, began spending winters basking in the waters, which were said to have curative powers. Later Tenakee Springs became known as Robber's Roost as illegal liquor, brothels, gambling and general lawlessness took over. After the marshals and citizens wrested control of the hamlet, peace reigned.

The springs are now housed in a community bathhouse on the waterfront, which has posted hours for men and women. (One of the town's biggest to-dos erupted over the fact that women had fewer allotted bath-hours than men, an unfairness that was remedied.)

The state ferry arrives once a week from Juneau (usually early in the morning) and twice from Sitka. Charter and scheduled air service from

Juneau and Sitka is available. Visitors can stay in a Victorian-style inn, bunkhouse or rental cabins. A couple of cafes serve good meals, and groceries and other supplies are sold at Snyder Mercantile (ask here about the cabins). An undeveloped campground on Indian River is two miles from town, but remember— this is bear country.

Visitors may enjoy hiking an 8-mile Forest Service trail along Tenakee Inlet, hunting, fishing, biking, or simply strolling along Tenakee Avenue chatting with locals and admiring their gardens.

Write to the city at: P.O. Box 52, Tenakee Springs, 99841 or call 736-2221.

Pelican

Pelican is forever linked with Rose's Bar and Grill. In fact, when the bar's namesake and owner, Rose Miller, sold the place and moved to Juneau in 1991, a delegation of fishermen tracked her down and begged her to come back. The bar just wasn't the same without her, they said. Rose went back.

Residents note that Pelican has other draws, particularly the spectacular scenery from its location on Lisianski Inlet nipped into the northwest coast of Chichagof Island. But Rose is one of those indelible characters, known for her splendid cooking, generosity and no-nonsense attitude. The Fourth of July is always a wild affair in Pelican, partly due to the influence of Rose's place and another saloon.

This is a fishing town founded by a fisherman in 1943. In fact, the community borrowed the name of his fish packer, *The Pelican*. The cold storage here processes the harvest from the nearby fishing grounds. The population, less than 300, grows during fishing seasons as boats swing in to unload their hauls and unwind themselves.

Visitors will have to work to get there. The ferry stops just twice monthly in the summer, but the two-hour layover is long enough for those who just want to look around. Scheduled air service from Juneau and Sitka is available as well. Services include rooms and a bed and breakfast, a cafe, a couple of bars and grocery and goods. The buildings loom over the tidelands on pilings. A fairly modern improvement was a boardwalk railing; previously, you weren't considered a true Pelicaner until you'd fallen off the boardwalk at least once. Visitors here may enjoy strolling the boardwalk, kayaking in picturesque Lisianski Inlet or along the coast, bird watching, fishing and other outdoor pursuits.

Write to the city at Box 757, Pelican 99832, or call 735-2202.

Hoonah

Hoonah largely keeps to itself. In its sheltered harbor at Port Frederick, ferry passengers often see just a glimpse of it during dockings at the Chichagof Island community. A Tlingit village occupied since before the Russians ever turned up, today old-fashioned frame homes cluster along the shoreline. Canneries and fishing sustain the economy, but subsistence food-gathering is a valuable part of daily life for the 900 residents.

Out-of-town hunters come to Hoonah to take advantage of the extended logging road system on Chichagof Island, but they should check first with the Forest Service to make sure the roads are open. Also offered is charter fishing. The village's location across Icy Strait from Glacier Bay makes it a launching point for boaters and kayakers.

A landing strip serves charter and scheduled air taxi, and a marina offers transient moorage. The state ferry visits twice weekly. Visitors will find a lodge, bed-and-breakfast rooms, a few restaurants, grocery stores and a gift shop with local arts and crafts. Attractions include the old cemetery near the ferry terminal, where Russian Orthodox crosses mark the lives of residents. Native artifacts are displayed in the town's cultural center. Good picnic spots are near the airport or at Cannery Point Beach.

Contact the city at 945-3663, or write to the U.S. Forest Service office at: Box 135, Hoonah, 99829. The agency sells a guide to area logging roads.

Tlingit Indians

L
ong before white explorers and colonists "discovered" Alaska, the
Tlingit Indians settled throughout the islands and coasts of Southeast
Alaska. Though archeologists are still trying to decipher the meaning of sites as old as 10,000 years, it is known that in more recent history,
Tlingits (pronounced "Klink-it" by non-Native speakers) existed here in a
complex and rich society divided by territory into "kwaans."

Anthropologist Wallace Olson's excellent guide to Tlingit culture and
history, *The Tlingit,* explains the meaning of kwaan as "people of that
place." Roughly a dozen such kwaans existed in recent times throughout
Southeast, with more than one village in each kwaan. Each village had
more than one clan, with their own crests, legends, and leaders. All Tlingits
belonged to one of two groups called moieties, represented by the raven
and the eagle. Tlingits fiercely defended their territories against each other
and against interlopers, and warfare was common.

The arrival of Russians and other whites had terribly harsh conse-
quences for the Tlingit people, not only as individuals but for the society
as a whole, which slowly changed under Western influence. Today, Native
leaders are working hard to revive their people's traditions, language, and
power. The kwaans became villages, and the Native inhabitants of these
communities are represented by village corporations organized in the 1971
Alaska Native Claims Settlement Act. The Sealaska Corp., based in Juneau, is the regional corporation, and all Tlingits belong as shareholders.

Tlingit social and cultural history is so densely elaborate with tradition, mythology, story, art, and family relations that such a brief mention
does it a major disservice. Suffice to say that travelers through Southeast

Alaska have many opportunities in each town to learn about the art, history, and social structure of the local Tlingits. It's worth remembering that historical accounts tend to reflect events as recorded by the colonizers, but that the Tlingit people had a very different perspective. All visitors need do is be respectful of Alaska's first inhabitants.

Two other Native cultures are represented in Southeast Alaska: the Haidas and the Tsimshians. The Haidas on Prince of Wales Island originally came a few centuries ago from the Queen Charlotte Islands, B.C. The Tsimshians of Metlakatla immigrated to Alaska with the Rev. William Duncan in the late 1800s.

A word about totem poles: Many are tempted to "read" totem poles, but, of course, it is much more complex than that. Crest poles relate the ancestry of a particular family. History poles reflect clan history. Legend poles relate stories or experiences. Memorial poles commemorate individuals. With crests, symbols, animals, faces and colors, poles signify many things. To fully appreciate individual poles, pick up brochures and booklets available in every town that help translate their nuances.

Tongass National Forest

As you glide past the forest covering the islands and mainland of the Inside Passage, remember that the public owns most of it. The 17-million-acre Tongass National Forest carpets nearly all of Southeast Alaska, stretching 500 miles long and 100 miles wide in spots. The largest public forest in the country, it is managed by the U.S. Forest Service. Just a small percentage of land in Southeast is owned by individuals, municipalities, the State of Alaska, or Native corporations that received parcels as part of the Alaska Native Claims Settlement Act.

Part of the Forest Service's job is to manage the Tongass for a variety of uses, including recreation, timber, mining, and wilderness. Just how to apportion those uses has been a source of incendiary controversy for the past couple of decades. Much of the debate centers around 50-year-long timber contracts awarded to pulp companies in Sitka and Ketchikan in the 1950s. Simply put, the main issue is jobs vs. old-growth forest. Many other terribly complex issues have arisen in recent years as the Forest Service revises its management plan to accommodate timber towns, outdoor enthusiasts, commercial fishermen, environmentalists, mining development, and the state and municipal interests.

For more information about the Tongass National Forest, write: Tongass National Forest, Information Center, 101 Egan Drive, Juneau, 99801. Information also is available from ranger district offices in Wrangell, Petersburg, Ketchikan, or Juneau. Forest Service staff often accompany sailings of the state ferry. These forest interpreters are knowledgeable about wildlife, forestry, and local conditions, and they welcome questions.

Wildlife Watching

Crews with the Alaska Marine Highway System like to call their ferries the world's greatest floating platforms for watching wildlife. From thedecks of a boat, passengers have an ideal vantage for spotting whales, porpoises, birds and even bears. Here are some wildlife-spotting tips:

WHALES: In Southeast you're most likely to see either humpback whales or orcas, also called killer whales. An estimated 300 to 250 humpbacks spend their summers in the cold waters of Southeast Alaska feeding on herring, bait fish and krill, which are tiny, shrimp-like crustaceans. Adult humpbacks can reach between 45 and 52 feet in length.

Look for spouts of moist air as they surface and exhale. You may hear a "whoosh" before you see the foggy exhalations. They travel rather slowly, their glossy backs rolling along just above the surface. When they dive, they arch their backs and then raise their distinctive 15-foot-long tail flukes high in the air before disappearing for several minutes. Researchers identify individual humpbacks by patterns on their flukes. You may also see their long pectoral fins, or flippers, rising from the water as they feed or play. A whale that throws itself out of the water is breaching; researchers believe there are several reasons for this behavior. Slaps, spy hops and tail lobbing are common, too. One of the humpback's most fascinating behaviors is bubble-net feeding, in which the whales, singly or in groups, blow nets of bubbles to trap their food and then scoop it up by lunging through it.

Orcas, which are really dolphins, are distinctive because of their tall dorsal fins, which jut sharply from the water. The male's fins are as much as six feet tall, larger than the female's. Orcas are sleek creatures with white ovals marking their black skin (one Forest Service interpreter calls them the "Maserati of the sea"). Despite their name, they have never been known to kill humans.

SEALS AND SEA LIONS: Both harbor seals and the larger Steller sea lions are common in Southeast waters. Seals average about 180 pounds. Male sea lions average about 1,200 pounds and 10 feet in length, with females slightly smaller. Though the two creatures can be difficult to tell apart in the water, seals have round heads and tend to float with just their large, liquid eyes above water. They sink under the surface quicker than you can blink. The doggish sea lion has a thick neck and pointed muzzle and tends to expose more of itself as it swims. Sometimes you will hear sea lions "grokking." In groups, they are playful, surging through the water and generally carrying on.

PORPOISES: You are likely to see both harbor and Dall porpoises, each quite different from the other. Harbor porpoises expose only their gray, rounded backs in a rolling motion as they cruise along. Dall porpoises create quite a commotion as they rip through the water, sending up spray and splashes. Often they will ride the bow waves of ships, always a thrill for passengers. They resemble orcas with their black-and-white coloring.

BALD EAGLES: Despite their graceful flight skills and noble appearance, eagles are really nothing more than scavengers. But who cares about that, right? They can soar for long minutes without beating their wings, which may span seven feet. Eagles reach maturity at about age five and are distinguished by their white heads and tails, dark bodies and golden beaks and feet. Immature eagles are entirely dark or have mottled feathers.

Look for eagles perched near the tops of trees, at the mouths of salmon streams during spawning season, or along beach driftwood at low tide. Often the white specks of their heads give them away first. With an estimated 10,000 eagles in Southeast, you will certainly spot some.

SEA OTTERS: No creature is more charming than the sea otter, and no fur was more coveted by the Russians. After nearly being wiped out in the 19th century, the otter populations are slowly recovering. In Southeast, you will encounter sea otters only along the outer coasts, near Sitka and

Glacier Bay. The inside waters are home to river otters.

BEARS: Both black and brown bears are shy (which is the way many visitors prefer it), but from the water you may spot them shambling along the shoreline. Keep a sharp eye out early in the morning and late in the evening, when they often wander the coast foraging for greens, scraping barnacles off rocks, or trying to snag spawning salmon along creeks. The two species can be difficult to tell apart, especially from a distance, as pelt color is really not a distinguishing factor. Look for the hump, dish face and greater size that characterize the brown, or grizzly bear, from the black bear. Remember that if you see a bear on Admiralty Island, you can be sure it's a brownie.

Too many species of birds and small mammals exist in Southeast to discuss here. For more information about Alaska's wildlife, the Alaska Department of Fish and Game offers a Wildlife Notebook Series with information about the natural history of the region's animals, birds and fish.

SUGGESTED READING

Reading about Alaska is almost as much fun as visiting it. (Almost.) Here's a suggested list of books about Southeast Alaska's history, wildlife, and culture.

The Nature of Southeast Alaska, by Rita M. O'Clair, Robert H. Armstrong, and Richard Carstensen. Bothell, Wa.: Alaska Northwest Books, 1992.

Guide to the Birds of Alaska, by Robert H. Armstrong. 2nd ed., Bothell, Wa.: Alaska Northwest Books, 1990.

The Founding of Juneau, by R. N. DeArmond. Juneau: Gastineau Channel Centennial Association, 1980.

Ketchikan, Alaska's Totemland, by Mary G. Balcom. Chicago: Adams Press, 1963.

Sitka, by Jack Calvin, illustrations by Dale DeArmond. 2nd ed., Sitka: Old Harbor Press, 1983.

The Tlingit: An Introduction to Their Culture and History, by Wallace M. Olson. Auke Bay: Heritage Research, 1991.

Skagway, Alaska, Gold Rush Cemetery, by Glenda J. Choate. Skagway: Lynn Canal Publishing, 1989.

Dolly's House: The Story of Alaska's Last Legal Madam & and Her Creek Street Home, by June Allen. 3rd ed., Ketchikan: Rainforest Publishing, 1991.

No Show Tonight, Katy Fulton. Petersburg: Pilot Publishing, Inc., 1992.

Alaska Geographic, a quarterly publication of the Alaska Geographic Society, has published more than 80 volumes focusing on particular cities, regions or resources of Alaska, including books on Skagway, Juneau, Glacier Bay, southern Southeast Alaska, Southeast Alaska, Admiralty Island, and more. Many issues are available in bookstores. For a complete list of volumes in print, write: The Alaska Geographic Society, P.O. Box 93370, Anchorage, 99509-3370.

147

NOTES

NOTES

Explore the West with
UMBRELLA BOOKS ™

CALIFORNIA LIGHTHOUSES, by Sharlene & Ted Nelson. A fascinating guide for travelers and historians to the more than 40 lighthouse stations that mark the California's 1,200 miles of meandering coastline, bays, and inland waterways from San Diego to the Redwood coast. $12.95, softbound, 192 pages

BICYCLING THE OREGON COAST, by Robin Cody. Explore the 370-mile route in nine unforgettable excursions. This comprehensive bicyclist's guide to the Oregon Coast includes useful maps with elevations given and details about attractions, people, places. $10.95, softbound, 128 pages.

NORTHWEST NATURAL HOTSPRINGS, by Tom Stockley. This guide to the most attractive natural hotsprings of Oregon, Washington, British Columbia and Alaska will make you want to jump into your car, boat, airplane, or snow machine — winter or summer — and race for the nearest hotsprings. $10.95, softbound, 96 pages.

INLAND NORTHWEST ANTIQUE STORES, by Bill London. Prize-winning traveler writer Bill London has written a humorous, anecdotal, fact-filled guide of the best antique stores in central and eastern Washington and north Idaho. $12.95, softbound, 160 pages.

THE INLAND EMPIRE (eastern Washington, north Idaho), by Bill London. This winner of a "Best Book" award from the Northwest Outdoor Writers Association introduces many of the colorful residents and much of the local lore through thirteen tours through eastern Washington and north Idaho. $10.95, softbound, 192 pages.

WASHINGTON LIGHTHOUSES, by Sharlene & Ted Nelson. The only guide available to Washington's 25 lighthouses. The historical accounts include entertaining, informative and humorous information about early light-keepers, as well as details on each light's status and accessibility. $10.95, softbound, 160 pages.

Send your order to: Epicenter Press, 18821 64th Ave. N.E., Seattle, WA 98155. Add $5 for first book, $3 for each additional book, for shipping and handling. Washington residents add 8.2% state sales tax on cover price.

MIKE MATHERS

ABOUT THE AUTHOR

Although Sherry Simpson has traveled throughout Alaska and has lived for several years in Fairbanks, Southeast Alaska remains her home. She arrived in Juneau with her family when she was seven and spent her high school years traveling to other communities on the state ferries as part of the girls' basketball team. She also lived in Petersburg. She graduated from the University of Alaska Fairbanks with a journalism degree and has worked for the Fairbanks *Daily News-Miner*, the *Juneau Empire*, and in television and public radio. She has written articles for several publications and is the author of Alaska Geographic's *Juneau*. She has won numerous state and regional journalism awards. Presently she is pursuing a master's degree in creative writing at the University of Alaska Fairbanks.